MAKERS
of the
MUSLIM
WORLD

Ahmad Riza Khan Barelwi

SELECTION OF TITLES IN THE MAKERS OF
THE MUSLIM WORLD SERIES

Series editor: Patricia Crone,
Institute for Advanced Study, Princeton

For current information and details of other books in the
series, please visit www.oneworld-publications.com/
subjects/makers-of-muslim-world.htm

MAKERS
of the
MUSLIM
WORLD

Ahmad Riza Khan Barelwi

In the Path of the Prophet

USHA SANYAL

ONEWORLD
OXFORD

AHMAD RIZA KHAN BARELWI

Oneworld Publications
(Sales and Editorial)
185 Banbury Road
Oxford OX2 7AR
England
www.oneworld-publications.com

ISBN 1–85168–359–3

Typeset by Jayvee, India
Cover and text designed by Design Deluxe
Printed and bound in India by Thomson Press Ltd
on acid-free paper

TO WILLIAM R. ROFF,

MY *USTAD*

CONTENTS

PREFACE

The subject of this book is an Indian Muslim scholar of the late nineteenth–early twentieth centuries, Ahmad Riza Khan Barelwi (1856–1921). His writings and the interpretation of Islam they espouse laid the foundation for a movement known to its followers as the Ahl-e Sunnat wa Jama'at ("the devotees of the Prophet's practice and the broad community") and to all others as "Barelwi," an adjective derived from Bareilly, the town where Ahmad Riza was born and where he lived. It also forms the last part of his name. The movement was one of several reformist groups to have emerged in British India during the late nineteenth century. Like their rivals, the Barelwis today have a large following in South Asia, as well as in Britain and other parts of the world where South Asian Muslims have migrated.

What distinguishes the Barelwis from the other reformist groups (Deobandis, the Ahl-e Hadith, and others) is their attitude to the relationship of the transcendant to this world. While the other groups reject sufism or Islamic mysticism either wholly or in part, and deny the importance of saintly mediators, miracles, and other manifestations of the holy in the here and now, the Barelwis embrace everything associated with sufism as an intrinsic part of their identity. But they share with the other reformists a strong focus on the Prophet Muhammad as a model of correct behavior and an example of the virtues that every Muslim should strive to cultivate and that he or she should live by.

Unlike some of the other Muslim reformist groups, Ahmad Riza defined religious community in cultural rather than political terms. When Indian Muslims began to engage in

of Deobandi world martial

xi

national politics in the early twentieth century, he advised his followers against it, arguing that the classical Islamic sources did not support political action against British rule in India, as the British had not interfered in the Muslims' internal affairs or religious institutions. This led to a split in the movement, with some Barelwi leaders following his advice and others rebelling.

In some respects, Ahmad Riza and the Barelwi movement in general seem paradoxical. Thus, while Ahmad Riza's interpretation of Islam was deeply rooted in South Asian culture, he based his arguments on the classical Islamic sources and looked to the religious leaders of Mecca and Medina for validation and approval. And while he was a reformist in the sense of demanding that his followers be personally responsible for their own salvation, the kind of model Muslim person he visualized was one who embraced rather than shunned ritual intermediaries and a ritualistic style of worshiping God. One might say that he wanted his followers to use reformist religious methods so as to be better, and more individually driven, traditionalists.

ACKNOWLEDGMENTS

Bill Roff, to whom I dedicate the book, guided the original Ph.D. dissertation on which this book is based, and has lent me his sage advice over many years even after he retired and returned to his home in Scotland. David Gilmartin has helped me think about the material in new ways which have found their way into this book. And Patricia Crone asked difficult questions and showed me that writing a little book can be harder than writing a big one. I would also like to thank the anonymous reviewer of the manuscript for making a number of suggestions which I have incorporated here.

I owe a great debt of gratitude to members of my family: my dear friend (and sister-in-law), Rupa Bose, who was my first reader and urged me to try and make the material both interesting and relevant to as wide an audience as possible. Gautam Bose, my husband, gave me time to write on weekends and holidays, while keeping our two boys, Girish and Arun (who are eight and six, respectively) entertained and out of mischief. And to my mother, Vina Sanyal, who has supported my academic endeavors in myriad ways over the years from far-away New Delhi, a heartfelt thank you.

Centers of Ahl-e Sunnat (Barelwi) Influence in the late 19th and early 20th centuries in North India

Lahore

DELHI

UNITED

Karachi

PROVINCES

Patna

Jabalpur

Calcutta

250 miles
500km

N

UNITED

Muradabad Rampur
DELHI Pilibhit
Bareilly
Badayun
Sitapur
Marahra Khairabad
Bilgram

PROVINCES

Kachhochha

Patna

Jabalpur

THE EIGHTEENTH- AND NINETEENTH-CENTURY BACKGROUND

In India, strong Muslim rule under the Mughal empire gave way in the course of the eighteenth century to weak central control and the establishment of a number of regional kingdoms which were independent of the Mughals in all but name. They in turn soon became indebted to the East India Company, which had started out as a trading company in 1600 but by the early nineteenth century had assumed a number of important political functions, the most important of which was the collection of land taxes. In 1858, after a failed Indian revolt against the East India Company, the British Crown assumed formal control of India and the East India Company was dissolved.

THE MUGHAL EMPIRE

For three centuries (1526 to 1857), India was ruled by the Mughals, who were Sunni Muslims of Central Asian descent. The founder of the empire was Babur (r. 1526–30), who swept into India from present-day Afghanistan, but whose brief reign left him no time to consolidate his gains in north India. It was his grandson Akbar (r. 1556–1605) who made a lasting impression on India and gave the empire a firm foundation. From their capital in the north (Delhi for the most part, though Akbar chose Agra and other cities as well), the Mughal emperors expanded the border in all directions. Starting from the northwest, including what are today Afghanistan and Pakistan, the empire expanded eastward to the Gangetic plain during Akbar's reign, going as far as what is today Bangladesh. To the north, the Himalayan mountains constituted a natural border, preventing further conquest in that direction. Central and southern India were ruled by independent kings, some Hindu, some Muslim, until well into Akbar's reign. In fact, the south was not incorporated into the Mughal empire until about a century later, during Aurangzeb's long reign (r. 1658–1707), and even then the very southern tip of India remained independent.

It was an agrarian empire, centered around the person and authority of the king. Land taxes constituted its main source of revenue. Since the majority of the Indian population was Hindu, during his fifty-year rule Akbar set about winning hearts and minds by including Hindu princes in all branches of government and even by marrying Hindu princesses. His eldest son, Salim (later Emperor Jahangir) had a Hindu mother, as did his grandson, Emperor Shah Jahan. At the same time, he showed his respect for popular Muslim religious figures. He paid homage to a particular lineage of Muslim mystics, or sufis, whose hospice was in the western Indian city of Ajmer. A story is told of how in 1570 he walked from his capital Fatehpur Sikri (near Agra), in the north, to Ajmer in the west, a distance of about two hundred miles, in a gesture of thanksgiving after the birth of his son Salim. Ajmer was the burial place of a thirteenth-century sufi whose intercession with God, the emperor believed, had been instrumental in his son's birth. In the first half of his reign, he also sponsored pilgrim ships from India's west coast to Mecca, sending generous gifts to that city. In sum, Akbar's religious eclecticism and inclusiveness helped

Indianize the foreign Mughals and strengthened and stabilized the empire. (In the second half of his reign, Akbar encouraged a personality cult around himself, inventing a new "religion" with elements of different faiths, alienating a number of Muslims as a result.)

Mughal decline began in the late 1600s during the reign of Akbar's great-grandson Aurangzeb (r. 1658–1707) and accelerated throughout the eighteenth century. Although historians argue about what caused the decline, a number of factors were at work: Aurangzeb's reversal of Akbar's religious policy is held by some to have been crucial, for he alienated a number of Hindu princely families by excluding them from positions of power and imposing on them a tax which Akbar had abolished (the *jizya*). In fact, the second half of Aurangzeb's reign was spent in incessant and, in the end, futile warfare against a minor Hindu chieftain, Shivaji (d. 1680), who eventually carved out a small kingdom along India's west coast and expanded it by warfare and diplomatic alliances with other Hindu rulers. In time, he and his successors (collectively known as the Marathas) were even able to challenge the Mughals in the north, the center of Mughal power. The financial drain of Aurangzeb's military campaigns on the empire's resources contributed to the collapse.

After Aurangzeb's death in 1707, the eighteenth century saw a succession of weak rulers. This encouraged foreigners to invade or try to take over. In 1739 the military general-turned-emperor Nadir Shah invaded north India from Persia in the west. Taking Lahore (now in Pakistan) in January of that year, he proceeded to march into Delhi a few months later. According to Juan Cole, "the savage looting of the capital later perpetrated by his troops constitut[ed] one of the century's great disasters" (1989: 41). The next major attack was launched by the Afghans, also from the northwest. In 1761, Ahmad Shah Abdali (later styled "Durrani") fought the Marathas at Panipat, fifty miles northwest of Delhi, where two important battles fought in earlier centuries had given the Mughals control over India. This, the Third Battle of Panipat, was won by Ahmad Shah, and could have led to Afghan rule over India had Ahmad Shah's troops not been weary of war and anxious to return home. The power vacuum in Delhi was soon to be filled by yet another foreign power, the British East India Company.

THE NORTH INDIAN SUCCESSOR STATES

Apart from the foreign threats to the Mughal empire in the eighteenth century, it was also subject to internal fissures. In north India, one of the most significant new developments was the rise of Shi'ism as the state religion in two of the largest Muslim successor states, Bengal and Awadh (known as "Oudh" in British sources). The kingdom of Awadh was founded by Burhan ul-Mulk in 1722 and was centered in Lucknow in the Gangetic plain. It grew in power under the first three governors or nawabs (Burhan ul-Mulk, Safdar Jang, and Shuja ud-Dawla) over the next fifty years. After Nadir Shah's invasion in 1739, the Mughal emperors were probably less powerful than the nawabs of Awadh. Although Shuja ud-Dawla, the third governor, stopped short of proclaiming Awadh's total independence from Mughal rule, continuing to mint coins in the emperor's name and having the Friday sermon read in his name, for all practical purposes the state operated independently. State affairs (diplomacy, economic policy, the appointment of officials and successors to the governorship) were conducted without reference to the Mughal emperor.

As both Cole and Francis Robinson (2001) explain, the culture of the Bengal and Awadh courts was fed by a constant influx of Shi'i Muslims from Iran and Iraq. Indeed, the governors of Awadh were themselves of Iranian (Nishapuri) origin.

This was a time of political instability in Iran as well, and Iranians and Iraqis of all professions were eager to seek their fortunes in either Bengal or Awadh. Spear speculates that had the British East India Company not intervened in India in the mid-1700s, the governors of both states would probably have tried to consolidate their power at the expense of the Mughals and/or each other, but would then have had to deal with the Marathas (Spear, 1981: 76–77). But British intervention prevented the playing out of this rather dismal scenario.

Despite Awadh's fairly rapid political decline in the latter part of the eighteenth century, Shi'ism continued to influence the political and cultural landscape of the eastern Gangetic plain throughout the eighteenth and nineteenth centuries. Indeed, at the end of the nineteenth century Ahmad Riza Khan wrote frequently about the negative influence of Shi'ism in his home territory of Rohilkhand, west of Lucknow, urging his followers to refrain from participating in Shi'i rituals and practices.

THE HISTORY OF ROHILKHAND

Closer to home for Ahmad Riza Khan and his family is the history of the Rohilla Afghans, after whom the region earned its name, Rohilkhand. The region around Bareilly, Ahmad Riza Khan's birthplace, was (and is) known as Rohilkhand, having been settled by the Rohilla Afghans in the seventeenth and eighteenth centuries. In the mid-eighteenth century Rohilkhand came under the authority of Hafiz Rahmat Khan (d. 1774) who was a forceful and strong leader who might have succeeded in making Rohilkhand a lasting regional power had there been fewer players vying for control over north India.

But this was not to be. Instead, the constant state of warfare finally forced the Rohillas to seek Awadh's help in order to beat back the Marathas. This in turn gave Awadh, under Shuja ud-Dawla, an excuse to take over in 1774 after Hafiz Rahmat Khan was killed in battle. Rohilkhand was thus absorbed into the state of Awadh. But by this time Awadh had become financially dependent on the East India Company (indeed, the latter had helped Awadh in its annexation of Rohilkhand). Consequently, in 1801 Awadh had to cede Rohilkhand to the East India Company as part repayment of its debt. It was to remain under Company rule until 1858, when India became a part of the British Empire and Rohilkhand became part of the new state known as the Northwest Provinces.   .

Economically, it is important to note, Rohilkhand had enjoyed considerable prosperity in the early period of its history under Afghan Rohilla rule. A rich alluvial plain in the foothills of the Himalayas, it was deemed one of the most fertile regions in the subcontinent in the early eighteenth century. But after it came under Awadh's rule, heavy revenue demands – made by Awadh in order to pay off its own debts to the East India Company – impoverished its people. Subsequently, similar demands by the East India Company led to indebtedness and rackrenting in the countryside.

Meanwhile, another facet of the political situation in the late eighteenth and early nineteenth centuries is of interest to us as part of Ahmad Riza Khan's family background, namely, the creation and growth of the independent state of Rampur, northwest of Bareilly. Rampur was the only Rohilla principality to survive the vicissitudes of the times and to continue to enjoy independence as a princely state under British rule. Rampur state was created by Faizullah Khan, who had fought by Hafiz Rahmat's side for over twenty years when the latter was killed in 1774, and had a reputation for bravery and leadership. Thus the mantle of leadership naturally fell to him.

However, as Rohilkhand had just been absorbed into Awadh, he had no territorial base of his own. Warren Hastings, then the

Governor of Bengal, concluded a treaty with him, granting him the small estate of Rampur (about 900 square miles) situated north of the city of Bareilly. Faizullah Khan thus became the first nawab of Rampur. Interestingly, although the Rampur nawabs' ancestors were Afghans – and Sunni Muslims – after the 1840s most of the Rampur nawabs were followers of Shi'ism.

By around 1800, the Marathas were no longer a threat in north India, having retreated to western India and split up into four separate confederate states, each of whom owed allegiance to the confederate chief or Peshwa in Pune. Bengal and Awadh had by now both come under the political and economic control of the East India Company: Bengal succumbed at the Battle of Plassey, thereby setting in motion East India Company rule over much of India for the next hundred years. Awadh, itself formally under Mughal rule, became increasingly indebted to the Company, and gradually, from 1775 to 1801, ceded parts of its territory to the British after Shuja ud-Dawla's death in 1774. Indirect rule over Awadh by the British was to continue until its formal annexation in 1856, a year before the Revolt.

BRITISH INDIA UNDER THE EAST INDIA COMPANY

If in the eighteenth century the British were one of several contenders for power in the wake of Aurangzeb's death and the weak rule of his successors, in the nineteenth they were unquestionably *the* most important power holders in India. This was not at all what they had intended, for the British had come to India as traders rather than as conquerers. The East India Company, formed in 1600, was but one of several European trading companies to come to India in search of "exotic" items of trade – chiefly spices, but also silks, fine handspun cottons, saltpetre (which had military uses), and other items. The other companies were Portuguese, Dutch, and French. The weakening of the Mughal empire in the first half of the eighteenth century coincided with European rivalries at home (during the Napoleonic wars, the War of Austrian Succession in the 1740s, and the Seven Years' War in the 1750s and 1760s) between the British and French, leading them into proxy wars in Bengal and south India. In the 1760s Robert Clive of the East India Company secured the *diwani* or revenue-collection rights to large parts of Bengal and Bihar, after driving the French out of south India. Gaining the right to the *diwani* was a milestone, for it allowed the British to pay for their purchases with Bengal's tax revenue, thereby making the annual export of bullion from Britain to India unnecessary.

Despite safeguards against abuse (for Clive and his men made small personal fortunes after their victories at Plassey and Buxar in the 1750s and 1760s) put in place by the Board of Directors in London, Company officials continued to enrich themselves personally until forbidden to engage in private trade in the 1790s. In 1813 missionaries and private traders were allowed into the country by an Act of Parliament, and in 1833 the Company lost its monopoly on trade in everything but opium and salt. Conquest of further territory, some direct and some indirect, followed swiftly during the first half of the nineteenth century. Under the pattern of indirect rule set in place by Clive, local rulers were allowed to retain their thrones but forced to concede to certain vital annual demands for revenue, which ultimately drove them into crippling debt to the Company. This in turn led, in due course, to the East India Company's assumption of political power.

A few dates will suffice to illustrate the pace of British annexation of territory, for these events are well known: in 1801 Madras Presidency was formed in the south, in 1803 the British defeated the Mughal emperor in Delhi and made him a pensioner, in 1818 parts of the Maratha confederacy were taken over to form the bulk of Bombay Presidency, in 1848 the Panjab was annexed, in the 1840s seven princely states were taken over in as many years under the Doctrine of Lapse (which forbade a ruler from choosing an adopted son as successor in the absence of a natural-born son and held that such a kingdom came under Company rule by default), and in 1856 the Nawab of Awadh was forced to give up his throne on grounds of incompetence.

In 1857–58, parts of the country rose in the anti-British rebellion known (in British accounts) as the Mutiny, though it was in fact much more broad-based than a mutiny, for it included peasants and landlords as well as soldiers. When the Revolt was finally put down in 1858, the anomaly of East India Company rule was replaced by the more normal mode of government called Crown rule, and the East India Company was dissolved. The last Mughal emperor, Bahadur Shah Zafar, was banished to Rangoon, Burma, where he lived out the rest of his days, after the British had murdered his sons to make sure there would be no heirs. (In an interesting parallel to this sad episode, in 1885 the ruler of Burma was banished to western India for the rest of his life after the British takeover of *that* kingdom.)

Economic Consequences of British Rule

Alongside the sweeping political changes indicated by these events were profound changes taking place in the areas under British control in the economic, legal, educational, and other spheres. The economic sphere was of course central to British concerns, and changes here began with the Permanent Settlement of Bengal in 1793. The British attempt to understand local land tenure systems was motivated by the desire to increase productivity and hence annual tax revenues – this being the *raison d'être* for the acquisition of territory by the Company. Seeing private property as the key to creating a class of "improving" landlords on the British model and hence to ensuring future agricultural productivity, in 1793 Lord Cornwallis, as Governor-General of Bengal, conferred private ownership rights in perpetuity on a number of Bengal *zamindars* or landlords, who were required in return to meet a "high and inflexible" annual revenue demand (Metcalf and Metcalf, 2002: 77).

However, the experiment failed. Under the indigenous system, the *zamindar* could "sell or transfer only his own revenue collecting rights, not the land itself, for that did not belong to him." If the peasants on his land felt overburdened, they could move to another part of the country where conditions were better. However, under the new system, all the *zamindars*, now owners of the land and liable to high taxes in good and bad years, were under an onerous burden themselves. Many were unable to pay the taxes and had no choice but to put their estates up for sale. Far from being improving landlords, a number of them sold their land to city-dwelling magnates who had the money to treat their estates as an investment (though without any incentive to "improve" them) at the tenants' expense. As for the tenants, they were reduced to the status of "tenants with no rights" (Metcalf and Metcalf, 2002: 77) and few options. Squeezed by the tax burden from above and unable to find better terms elsewhere (as all the landlords now enforced the same high revenue demand), in time they became a class of landless bonded labor. A third of the estates are believed to have changed hands in the first twenty years following the Settlement of 1793.

In the years ahead, various alternatives were tried in other parts of India, ranging from assessments being revised every twenty or thirty years to ownership being fixed on the tenants (*ryots*) rather than the landlords, in south India. Meanwhile, new crops were introduced in Bengal and elsewhere. A highly profitable trade in opium was started in Bengal in the 1820s for export to China. This complicated three-way trade allowed the Company to pay for its exports from China with the proceeds of opium sales in China, once again making unnecessary the export of bullion from Britain. Opium "provided up to 15 per cent of the Indian Government's total revenue" in the 1830s (Metcalf and Metcalf, 2002: 75).

Another important economic change in India in the early 1800s was the substitution of factory-made British textiles for handmade Indian cloth, which put Indian weavers in Bengal out of work and increased pressure on the land. The destruction of the textile industry followed – British-made textiles being cheaper to buy than the local product – initiating "the development of a classically 'colonial' economy, importing manufactures and exporting raw materials, [in a pattern] that was to last for a century, until the 1920s." The Metcalfs conclude, "Overall, ... the East India Company during the early decades of the nineteenth century did little to set India on a path of economic growth" (Metcalf and Metcalf, 2002: 75, 76).

Improvements in Infrastructure

While the economy was dramatically affected in these and other ways during the early nineteenth century, infrastructural developments had a lasting impact on Indians of all classes and communities. Railroads and the telegraph were introduced during Lord Dalhousie's governor-generalship in the 1850s, and a postal system and print technology were introduced, making newspapers and periodicals available relatively cheaply. To give but one example of how significant a change the "penny post" represented, "[i]n the 1830s an exchange of letters between Britain and India could take two years; by 1870, with the opening of the Suez Canal [in the 1860s], a letter could reach Bombay in only one month" (Metcalf and Metcalf, 2002: 97). Print technology, as we will see in subsequent chapters, greatly facilitated the growth of Islamic (as well as other religious) reform movements in the latter half of the nineteenth century.

Change was occurring in almost every area of life at this time. From the point of view of the north Indian 'ulama, two areas were particularly significant, namely, education and the law.

A British Model for India

Having become the colonial masters of India, the British had to decide what direction they wanted the country to take. What was the British purpose in being in India, what did it hope to achieve other than the economic and imperial goals of hegemony? Answering this question also involved assessing the Indian past. Did those who now governed India see anything of value in India's linguistic and literary heritage, its educational traditions, its legal texts, and so on, or should Britain set in place a wholly Western system, a wholly new set of institutions that had no local roots whatsoever?

This debate played out most famously in the fields of law and education. Among those who spoke for the liberal position (the term meant something different in the 1800s than it does in US politics in the early twenty-first century) were Lord William Bentinck, Governor-General of India in the late 1820s and early 1830s, and John Stuart Mill who worked for the East India Company from 1823 until 1858. Mill argued that different peoples were at different stages in the "ladder" of "progress" but could be advanced along the way by means of education and good government. Charles Trevelyan, who served in India in the

1830s, was also among this group. He believed that British learning and institutions would put India on the path to "moral and political improvement" (Metcalf, 2001: 28–33). Thomas B. Macaulay is perhaps the best-known example of this position. In a well-known statement in 1835, he said he wanted to put in place a system of education which would "create not just a class of Indians educated in the English language, who might assist the British in ruling India, but one 'English in taste, in opinions, in morals and in intellect'" (Metcalf, 2001: 34).

As Thomas Metcalf points out, this view was based on the belief that all "races" were inherently educable and none had to remain perpetually on the lowest rung of the ladder of "civilization." But it was also based on a negative assessment of non-European cultures and their traditions of learning. Thus Macaulay is famous for his dismissal of the "entire literature of India and Arabia ... [as worth less than] a single shelf of a good European library" (Metcalf, 2001: 34). This negative assessment of India stood in contrast with the views of an earlier generation of officials and scholars such as Governor-General Warren Hastings and Sir William Jones, a judge in the East India Company (d. 1794), who believed that India's rich textual tradition was worthy of study by Europeans (which in turn required the study of languages, chiefly Sanskrit, but also Arabic for an understanding of Muslim texts), and that the British could best rule by basing their laws on those of the country itself.

"The outcome of British study of the ancient texts, in Jones's view," Metcalf writes, "was to be a 'complete digest' of the Hindu and Muslim law, which could be enforced in the Company's courts, and would preserve 'inviolate' the rights of the Indian people" (Metcalf, 2001: 12). It was in this spirit – as well as a desire to be independent of Brahmin interpreters he considered unreliable – that Jones worked on his *Digest* (Metcalf, 2001: 24). It was published in 1798 by his successor

H. T. Colebrooke. To be sure, Jones also graded European and "Oriental" learning and their laws on a hierarchical scale in which the European was superior to the Indian. Furthermore, in his view of things, India's glorious past or "golden age" had given way to a state of decline in the present. Nevertheless, he differed fundamentally from Macaulay and others of like mind who devalued and belittled the Sanskritic and Arabo-Persian literary traditions altogether, and who sought to base British laws and education in India on Western traditions alone.

In the end, Macaulay and Mill carried the day, though without totally rejecting Hastings' and Jones' vision. Since 1772 civil law had been based on religious affiliation, for Hindus and Muslims were governed by their own personal laws – Hindu law for the former, and "Anglo-Mohammadan" law for Muslims. In practice, the manner in which Islamic law was implemented was much altered under the East India Company. As Zaman shows, certain medieval texts deemed authoritative by the British were "invested with almost exclusive authority as the basis of judicial practice in British courts, as far as Muslim personal law was concerned" (Zaman, 2002: 22). Moreover, the manner of their application was more rigid than it had been in Mughal times, in keeping with the British desire to impose uniformity and predictability in the law. (Zaman points out that the British were inconsistent in their application of the law too, but this was described as exercising "discretion" rather than being "arbitrary.")

Macaulay was instrumental, in the 1860s, in drafting a new penal code which replaced what the British saw as despotic "Oriental" rule with "predictable rules and regulations for the adjudication of disputes." Based on Jeremy Bentham's principles of utilitarianism, the new laws also sought to promote "unity, precision, and simplicity" (Metcalf, 2001: 37, 38). Islamic criminal law ceased to be applied in the courts after this time. Moreover, the muftis (and Brahmin pandits) who had been employed to help British judges on matters of personal religious law were no longer deemed necessary, and the position of "native law officer" was abolished in 1864. Qadis (judges who applied Islamic law) were frequently not appointed to British Indian courts either. Thus the application of Anglo-Muhammadan law in British Indian courts was often in the hands of non-Muslim judges. This made even simple matters such as the dissolution of a marriage, for example, impossible, as such a decision was invalid in Muslim eyes if made by a non-Muslim judge (Zaman, 2002: 25, 27). In the nineteenth century the Deobandi 'ulama tried unsuccessfully to create an alternative court of their own, but for a variety of reasons many Muslims continued to use the British Indian courts (Metcalf, 1982: 147). As we shall see throughout this book, the primary response of the 'ulama to the loss of access to the courts under British rule was to issue responsa (fatawa). The other alternative was to take the issue under dispute to a Muslim princely state where British laws were not in place and where a qadi could be found.

Education was also a significant issue for the 'ulama during British rule. During the late eighteenth century, Orientalist scholars such as William Jones had promoted schools for the education of maulwis and pandits who could assist Company officials in the interpretation of Hindu and Muslim law, respectively. Among the best-known schools of this period were the Calcutta Madrasa (founded in 1781), the Sanskrit College in Benares (founded in 1792), and Delhi College, which had originated as a madrasa during Aurangzeb's reign. Although the focus in all these schools was on "Oriental" learning, Delhi College also taught its students Western sciences and mathematics through works translated from English into Urdu. In addition, Lord Wellesley, Governor-General from 1798 to 1805, established the College of Fort William in Calcutta in 1800 to teach young British recruits to the Company Indian languages and Hindu and Muslim law, as well as Western sub-jects, before sending them out into the countryside as adminis-trators. Less well known is the College at Fort St. George, Madras, founded in 1812 by Francis Ellis, which trained the British in Indian languages and Indians in Hindu and Muslim law simultaneously (Cohn, 1996: 47–53).

When this Orientalist approach gave way, from the 1820s, to the supporters of "reform" and "liberalism," the purpose of education became to instil British values. In 1835 Macaulay wrote in his policy statement or "Minute on Education" that the goal of British education in India should be to create a class of Indians who would be "English in taste, in opinions, in morals and in intellect." If this meant that down the road they would also want self-rule – as he thought they must – this was to be welcomed, for the new political order would be one that represented "an imperishable empire of our arts and our morals, our literature and our laws" (Metcalf and Metcalf, 2002: 81). In any event, this was a distant prospect, not something that British policy makers needed to worry about there and then.

The immediate consequences of Macaulay's educational blueprint included, in 1835, the substitution of English for Persian as the language of government. Under the reform-minded Governor-General, Lord Bentinck (1828–35), several colleges were founded, though no effort was made to set up elementary schools. In Britain at this time, schools were run by parochial (religious) bodies, not by government. Among the universities that date to this period are Patna College. Elphinstone College was founded in the 1820s in Bombay. Hindu College in Calcutta had been established in 1819, with private British and Indian financial support. By the 1830s English was being avidly studied by "several thousand Indians" in Calcutta alone (Metcalf and Metcalf, 2002: 82). The first three Indian universities were inaugurated in 1857.

This embrace of Western learning was but an aspect of a wider reform movement under Raja Ram Mohan Roy, founder of the Brahmo Samaj in Calcutta, who sought to reform the Hinduism of his day in the light of a perceived golden age accessed through the study of ancient Sanskrit texts. That earlier form of Hinduism, for Roy, was characterized by rationalism and simplicity rather than the idol worship of contemporary times. David Kopf has characterized this era as the "Bengal Renaissance" on account of its spirit of enquiry and its openness to reinterpretation of received tradition (Kopf, 1969).

2

THE MUSLIM RESPONSE

Indians of all religions were keenly aware of Western criticisms of their religious customs and traditions. The Hindu reformer Raja Ram Mohan Roy had responded by rejecting many aspects of contemporary ritual practice, arguing that the "pure" Hinduism of India's "golden age" was rational, simple, and devoid of practices which the British described as barbaric (such as idol worship, caste, widow immolation, child marriage, and other social practices deemed detrimental to women). He also considered certain Sanskritic texts authoritative, and advocated their study as a means of reforming religious and social practices.

In the Muslim case, religious leaders in the eighteenth and nineteenth centuries promoted internal reform as a response to Britain's rule of India. They reasoned that if Muslims had lost political power after so many centuries of rule, it was because they had been religiously negligent. Had they been "good" Muslims, they would have been strong and the British would never have been able to take over. Specifically, Muslim reformers advocated greater individual adherence to religious precepts as set out in the shari'a, greater knowledge of the religious texts by the 'ulama and, to some degree, by ordinary believers, and a focus on the Prophet as a model of behavior in one's daily life. A related concern was with preaching (*dawa*), mainly to other Muslims, to encourage greater religiosity. Their attitudes toward two other questions – sufism (Islamic mysticism) and British rule – varied widely. On both issues we find everything from complete acceptance to total rejection.

The reformers' emphasis on authoritative texts, namely, the Qur'an which Muslims regard as the literal word of God, and secondarily the traditions of the Prophet (hadith), led to the first translations of the Qur'an. The Qur'an is learned and memorized in the original Arabic, but in India Muslims spoke Persian in the eighteenth and early nineteenth centuries, or Urdu starting in the mid-nineteenth century, or a regional Indian language such as Bengali or Tamil. Because Arabic was not spoken by Indian Muslims, the Qur'an was poorly understood. Muslim reformers in the late eighteenth and nineteenth centuries translated the Qur'an into Persian, and much later into Urdu and other Indian languages.

The Indian reform movements also highlighted the hadith literature. The hadith are narratives (literally, stories or news reports) about the Prophet (d. 632), relating to something he did or said, or which tell about his appearance, comportment, and so on. These narratives were orally transmitted by his followers to successive generations of Muslims before being written down about a century after his death. A laborious process of evaluation over two centuries eventually resulted in six collections of hadiths, named after the jurists who had collected them. The collection regarded as the most reliable is that of al-Bukhari (d. 870), with that of Muslim (d. 875) the next most reliable.

The focus of the hadith literature is the Prophet, and all the Indian Muslim reform movements of the eighteenth and nineteenth centuries were united in their strong emphasis on the personality and biography of the Prophet. They saw in him a model for how they could, and should, live their own lives. This made him an example one could hope to emulate. Together with the Qur'an becoming a subject of scholarly discussion and interpretation, the view of the Prophet as a model Muslim meant that the 'ulama, and through their leadership other Muslims, were individually responsible for fulfilling their religious obligations as Muslims and relying much less than before on intermediaries and socially accepted, customary ways of behavior. This characteristic unites all the reform movements, despite their great diversity in other ways.

While the political dominance of the British in India, and their debates about the intrinsic value or lack thereof of "Oriental" learning, were a powerful impetus for reform among Indian Muslims, there was also another source which came from the Islamic world itself, namely, the Wahhabi movement in eighteenth- and nineteenth-century Arabia. The influence of this movement on Indian reform movements was felt through the annual pilgrimage to Mecca, through extensive periods of study by a small number of Indian Muslims at Mecca and Medina, and by the general improvement in communications which occurred in the eighteenth and nineteenth centuries. The founder of the Wahhabi movement was Muhammad ibn 'Abd al-Wahhab (1703–87). His message was an insistence on the unity of God (tawhid), which meant that all forms of superstition (the veneration of saints' tombs, holy objects, and the like) were contrary to the worship of the one God. He believed that the first generation of Muslims, namely, the Prophet and his companions, were the models of true Islamic practice. He therefore rejected later developments in the history of Islam, particularly sufism and what he viewed as its excesses. Albert Hourani (1983: 37) describes his ideas as follows:

> The true Islam, stated Ibn 'Abd al-Wahhab, was that of the first generation, the pious forerunners, and in their name he protested against all those later innovations which had in fact brought other gods into Islam: against the later development of mystical thought, with its monist doctrines, its ascetic renunciation of the goods of the world, its organization into brotherhoods, its rituals other than those prescribed by the

Quran; against the excessive cult of Muhammad as perfect
man and intercessor with God (although great reverence was
paid to him as Prophet); against the worship of saints and
reverence for their shrines; and against the return into Islam
of the customs and practices of the [pre-Islamic age].

Although the precise influence of Ibn 'Abd al-Wahhab on
Indian Muslim reformers of the eighteenth and nineteenth
centuries is a matter of scholarly debate, there is no doubt that
his ideas were well known and that they played a major role in
the thought of some religious thinkers in India.

SHAH WALI ULLAH

In the eighteenth century, the figure of Shah Wali Ullah Dehlawi
(1703–62) stands out as preeminent. The progressive collapse
of central authority in Delhi caused him to plead with Muslim
leaders in Rohilkhand and in south India to do something to
restore order. In his anxiety to see a strong Muslim ruler, Shah
Wali Ullah even invited Ahmad Shah Abdali of Afghanistan to
invade and take over. He must have been pleased with the outcome of the Battle of Panipat in 1761, which resulted in Ahmad
Shah's victory over the Marathas and held out the hope of stable
central government from Delhi. But he died the next year, and
as we know, that battle did nothing to settle the question of central rule as Abdali returned to Afghanistan, leaving a power vacuum in his wake.

However, Shah Wali Ullah is remembered chiefly for his contribution to religious rather than political matters. His father,
Shaikh 'Abd ur-Rahim (1644–1718), had established a seminary or madrasa, the Madrasa-i Rahimiyya, in Delhi, and this
was where he spent his lifetime – as director of the school, as
teacher, and as thinker and writer. His chief contribution to
Islamic studies was to insist on the importance of the study of

hadith (pronounced *hadis* in Urdu), the traditions of the Prophet, and to argue that the 'ulama had an obligation to study the original sources (the Qur'an and hadith) and draw on all four Sunni schools of law (*madhhab*, pl. *madhahib*) eclectically to make legal judgments.

The four Sunni law schools (Shi'i Muslims have three of their own) came into being around the late tenth century. Named after their founders, they are geographically based, such that different parts of the Muslim world have come over time to be associated with one or other of the four. In India, the predominant school is the Hanafi, named after Abu Hanifa of Iraq (d. 767). The schools are distinguished by minor differences of judgment between them. In this book, for example, we will see the case of a scholar combining the judgments of two different schools of law in a case relating to apostasy and marriage. However, most Indian Muslim scholars (including Ahmad Riza), frowned upon such practice.

The founding of the four law schools had the general effect of making it unnecessary for jurists to go directly to the sources (the Qur'an and the prophetic traditions), allowing them to rely instead on the judgments of the founding jurists on major issues. Muslim scholars metaphorically refer to this development as the "closing of the gate of *ijtihad*," or independent reasoning. Thus, once the medieval jurists had judged something to be forbidden or permitted, based on the guidance of the Qur'an and prophetic traditions, all that later generations of scholars had to do was to follow in their footsteps. They no longer had to consult the original sources themselves.

But while this was generally the case, in fact independent reasoning never ceased as new issues constantly arose, needing fresh interpretation and judgment by the 'ulama. Shah Wali Ullah contributed to Islamic reform in eighteenth-century India by reminding the Indian 'ulama of their obligation to make legal judgments in light of the original sources, choosing between the judgments of the four schools when they deemed this to be necessary, rather than following the one that was customary in their part of the world. "His espousal of jurisprudential eclecticism combined with consultation of Qur'an and *hadis* clearly enhanced the responsibility of the 'ulama for interpreting the Law to their followers" (Metcalf, 1982: 38). It is important to note, however, that this obligation was limited to the learned, the *khawass*, to the exclusion of the ordinary (*'amm*) believer. Most Muslims, including most 'ulama, were urged to follow Hanafi law exclusively; only a few were encouraged to engage in *ijtihad* along the lines indicated.

In Islamic terms, the study of hadith is part of the branch of study known as *manqulat*, or the traditional sciences (from the Arabic root *nql*, to transmit, hand down), in contrast with the *ma'qulat* or the "rational" sciences (cf. Arabic *'aql*, meaning reason, rationality) which include subjects such as philosophy. Shah Wali Ullah's espousal of the traditional sciences stands in contrast to other schools of religious scholars (including Ahmad Riza Khan) to be discussed shortly. In his view, the rational sciences were a source of confusion and should be avoided. The study of hadith, on the other hand, would bring Muslims closer to the sources of their tradition and thereby strengthen and unite the community. Likewise, he encouraged the 'ulama to study the Qur'an directly as well, and to this end he translated it from Arabic into Persian. At the time, this was an act of great courage which elicited much criticism from the 'ulama.

Shah Wali Ullah is also known for his contributions to a major issue in sufism, namely, the theory of the unity of being (*wahdat al-wujud*) versus the unity of witness (*wahdat al-shuhud*). This debate had been ongoing among sufis in India since the seventeenth century. The *wujudi* position is identified with Ibn al-'Arabi (d.1240), the famous Andalusian sufi of the thirteenth century. Ibn al-'Arabi had argued that creation has no empirical existence in and of itself, that it is but an aspect of God Himself. It follows logically from this position that human beings themselves are but an emanation of God, not independent of Him. Critics of this theory, of which there were many, argued that this position denies *tawhid*, the Oneness of God, for it makes humans the partners of God. Shah Wali Ullah's view on this subject was to argue that the two positions were less at variance with one another than is commonly believed. "The whole universe is pervaded by a common exist-ence, he argued, an existence both immanent and transcen-dent, but beyond that existence is the Original Existence of God" (Metcalf, 1982: 40). However, Shah Wali Ullah believed that the subject was too subtle to be discussed publicly, and he urged caution in the matter. According to Metcalf, his espousal of the *wujudi* position led to its wide acceptance by later gener-ations of Indian sufis.

Shah Wali Ullah also sought to reconcile Sunni and Shi'i Muslims, at a time of increased Shi'a influence in the regional courts at Awadh and Bengal. He venerated 'Ali, as did the Shi'i, but held that the first two caliphates (those of Abu Bakr and 'Umar) were superior to the last two (those of 'Uthman and 'Ali), because the Muslims had been politically united during their rule. Although this attempt at bridge-building was not very successful, Shah Wali Ullah's achievements in other respects – his emphasis on hadith studies, his scholarly output as an 'alim, and his high attainments as a sufi – were remarkable. Particularly important was his role in renewal of the law, as demonstrated by his emphasis on *ijtihad*. In the fol-lowing century, his work was continued by his four sons, espe-cially Shah 'Abd ul-Aziz, whom the Ahl-e Sunnat regarded as the Renewer of the thirteenth Islamic century.

FARANGI MAHALL: TRAINING EMPLOYEES FOR THE MUSLIM STATES

While Shah Wali Ullah taught and wrote from his Madrasa-i Rahimiyya in Delhi, another group of Sunni 'ulama, known as the Farangi Mahallis, were making their mark in Lucknow at the same time. Their residence in Lucknow began when, in 1695, Emperor Aurangzeb granted the four sons of Mulla Qutb ud-Din (d. 1692) the house of a European merchant (hence the name "Farangi Mahall," or foreigner's house) in recompense for their father's murder and loss of the family's library to arson. In the eighteenth century the third son, Mulla Nizam ud-Din, devised a new madrasa curriculum which came to be known as the Dars-i Nizami. Madrasas all over India gradually adopted this syllabus. The madrasa at Farangi Mahall became a center for learning on a par with the Madrasa-i Rahimiyya.

Unlike the latter, the Farangi Mahall madrasa focused on *ma'qulat* or rational studies. Francis Robinson, who has made an exhaustive study of the Farangi Mahall 'ulama, shows in detail the differences between the curricula followed by the two madrasas. Where the Madrasa-i Rahimiyya emphasized hadith, the Farangi Mahall curriculum emphasized grammar, logic, and philosophy (Robinson, 2001: 46–53). The Farangi Mahall 'ulama believed that knowledge of these sciences was "crucial to the study of legal theory and jurisprudence (*usul al-fiqh*) and of theology (*'ilm al-kalam*), and expertise in them helped make many ... other disciplines accessible" (Zaman, 2002: 76). They also de-emphasized the study of sufism. The reason, Robinson explains, was that the 'ulama at Farangi Mahall were seeking to train future

lawyers, judges and administrators ... [whose] skills were in demand from the increasingly sophisticated and complex bureaucratic systems of seventeenth- and eighteenth-century India. ... The emphasis of the [curriculum] on training

capable administrators for Muslim states rather than
specialists in "religion" *per se* may explain the dropping
of mysticism from the course. Knowledge of Sufism was
not what trainee administrators wanted. (Robinson,
2001: 53)

In practice, the curriculum was flexible within the overall
framework initially set out by Mulla Nizam ud-Din. Zaman
writes,

Only in the latter half of the nineteenth century, and ...
possibly in response to a certain measure of influence
exercised by Western styles and institutions of education in
British India, did the Dars-i Nizami acquire a more or less
standardized form that was widely adopted as a "curriculum"
by madrasas of the Indian subcontinent. Madrasas have
continued, however, to differ in their versions of this
curriculum, which has scarcely been impervious to change
even after its standardization in the late nineteenth century.
(Zaman, 2002: 68)

The point that the curriculum of the Dars-i Nizami was more
rather than less flexible *before* British influence made itself felt is
interesting and worth noting. (It also accords with what historians know of a host of other Indian institutions, such as caste
itself, which became relatively "fixed" and inflexible in practice
in the later nineteenth century.)

However, if the purpose of the Dars-i Nizami was to train
Muslim bureaucrats to work in the Indian Muslim states in the
late eighteenth century, the political instability of the Muslim
successor states made the princes rather undependable as
patrons for prospective qadis (judges in Islamic law courts) or
muftis ('ulama qualified to issue fatawa [sing. fatwa], juridical
responses). The same may be said for those whose skills lay in
writing poetry, in the musical arts, or even in the military, for

that matter. Metcalf writes as follows about the difficulties Farangi Mahallis encountered at this time:

> Wherever there was a prince, the Farangi Mahallis sought positions under him. Thus in the mid-eighteenth century ... three members of the family joined princely armies. The travels, the varieties of employment, the violent deaths of at least one member in each of the first four generations of the family – all this suggests the difficulties facing the family in maintaining the pattern of dependence on princes. (Metcalf, 1982: 32)

NINETEENTH-CENTURY REFORM MOVEMENTS

The nineteenth-century reformists, of which there were many groups, shared in the broad set of goals indicated earlier, namely, better knowledge of the textual sources of Islam (mainly through the creation of new seminaries for the training of scholars), greater adherence to religious precepts by individual believers, and a close modeling of their lives on that of the Prophet. However, they differed in significant ways. Based on their attitude toward British rule, we can distinguish three broad groups: the vast majority (Shah 'Abd ul-'Aziz, the Deobandis, the Ahl-e Hadith, the Nadwat al-'Ulama, the Ahmadis) were relatively uninterested in participating in the opportunities being opened up by British rule, although most of them accepted it without active protest. Of this group, the Ahl-e Hadith were the least accommodating toward the British while the Nadwa and the Ahmadis were the most so. The jihadists (Sayyid Ahmad Barelwi and his followers), on the other hand, were actively opposed not only to British rule but to all forms of non-Muslim rule. They sought to restore Muslim rule through political means, fighing the Sikhs in the Panjab, and the British in northwest India generally. The Faraizi movement in Bengal falls in between the two, in that although the Faraizis did not declare a jihad against the British, they boycotted British-run institutions and refused to pay land taxes. Finally, the accommodationists (Sayyid Ahmad Khan) embraced British rule as a positive good from which Indian Muslims stood to benefit.

Ahmad Riza belongs to the first group, though his story is not addressed until the following chapter.

Shah 'Abd ul-'Aziz

After Shah Wali Ullah's death in 1762, his eldest son Shah 'Abd ul-'Aziz (d. 1824) took over the management of the Madrasa-i Rahimiyya. Shah 'Abd ul-'Aziz followed in the footsteps of his illustrious father by studying and promoting hadith scholarship, but widened the circle of those he addressed through the number of fatawa he wrote for individual Muslims who sought his advice. The subject matter of the fatawa ranged widely from details regarding the proper way to perform the ritual prayer to relations with Shi'i Muslims, and to whether it was legitimate to seek employment under the British. The increased importance of fatwa writing was a direct result of the loss of political power by Muslims, which led to a greater need for personal guidance by the 'ulama, now that they no longer had state-based shari'a courts.

One fatwa by Shah 'Abd ul-'Aziz has been particularly commented upon by later historians on account of its political implications. In 1803, he was asked whether it was permissible for a Muslim to give and take interest under British rule. The date is important, for Delhi had been occupied by the East India Company that year. Would he take foreign occupation and the suspension of religious law in parts of the country to mean that the normal rules of conduct in other spheres of Muslim life no longer applied either? His answer to this question was equivocal. In a land ruled by Muslims (termed *dar ul-Islam* in Islamic law), interest (*sud*, or, in Arabic, *riba*) is prohibited. However, in the troubled circumstances of the early nineteenth century, many Muslims had fallen on hard times and were deeply in debt. If Shah 'Abd ul-'Aziz were to judge on the basis of the Islamic sources of law (Qur'an, hadith, and the principles of analogy [*qiyas*], and community consensus or *ijma*) that the legal status of British-controlled territory had changed (or, in Islamic terms, that it was *dar ul-harb* rather than *dar ul-Islam*), the prohibition on taking and receiving interest could be temporarily suspended.

Shah 'Abd ul-'Aziz's response to the question was that in Delhi at that time, "the *Imam al-Muslimin* [the leader of the Muslims, perhaps a reference to the Mughal emperor] wields no authority, while the decrees of the Christian leaders are obeyed without fear [of retribution]. ... From here to Calcutta the Christians are in complete control" (Metcalf, 1982: 46; my interpolation in square brackets). While he did not directly say that the legal status of Delhi had changed from the abode of Islam to that of war, he implied that it had, so that he could be understood as tacitly permitting the questioner to engage in interest-bearing transactions without incurring sin (Mushir ul-Haqq, 1969). Or, to put it another way, "'Abdu'l-'Aziz thus appears to have wanted Muslims to behave politically as if the situation were daru'l-islam, for he gave no call to military action [against the British], yet he wanted them to recognize that the organization of the state was no longer in Muslim hands" (Metcalf, 1982: 51).

This fatwa is particularly interesting because of the way it has been interpreted by Muslims in the twentieth century. It has been read – by Muslim nationalists as well as Muslim nationalist historians – as an endorsement of jihad (holy war) against the British. Their reasoning is that if it was no longer a sin to take on interest-bearing debt, it could only mean that the country was under non-Muslim rule, which in turn meant that holy war was justified against it. However, Metcalf suggests that Shah 'Abd ul-'Aziz may even have opposed the jihad that was launched shortly before his death. At any rate, he is known to have encouraged his nephew and son-in-law 'Abd ul-Hayy to accept a job offered to him by the East India Company – further evidence, it would seem, that he did not endorse jihad. However that may be, a jihad movement was launched in 1830 by Sayyid Ahmad of Rae Bareli (a town in Awadh). To him we may now turn.

Sayyid Ahmad Barelwi

Sayyid Ahmad Barelwi (not to be confused with Ahmad Riza Khan Barelwi, the subject of this book) was born in 1786 to a family that claimed descent from the Prophet Muhammad. Among Muslims, such families (known by the title "Sayyids") enjoy high status by virtue of their ancestry. He traveled as a young man from his hometown to Lucknow in search of work, and then to Delhi, where he studied under Shah 'Abd ul-Qadir (Shah 'Abd ul-'Aziz's brother) of the Madrasa-i Rahimiyya from 1805 to 1811. Thereafter he left for central India, where he served as a cavalryman for one Amir Khan who worked for the Marathas. In 1818, this Amir Khan was "forced to come to terms with the British who [awarded] him the principality of Tonk and styled him a *nawwab*" (Metcalf, 1982: 54).

Sayyid Ahmad then returned to Delhi the second time, now as a religious reformer determined to bring about greater observance of the shari'a. Some prominent younger members of the Shah Wali Ullah family accepted him as their spiritual leader (sufi shaikh). His ideas are set out in two influential books by his close associate Muhammad Isma'il (d. 1831).

Entitled *Taqwiyat al-Iman* (Strengthening the Faith) and *Sirat al-Mustaqim* (The Straight Path), the first was published in Persian, but soon translated into Urdu, while the second was actually written in Urdu. The central theme of the *Taqwiyat al-Iman* is the claim that the Muslims of the time had deviated from the principle of *tawhid*, strict monotheism, by a number of objectionable practices representing a form of *shirk* (associationism or polytheism, the opposite of *tawhid*). He divides them into three main groups, associating some with God's knowledge (*ishrak fi'l 'ilm*), others with God's power (*ishrak fi'l tasarruf*), and others with God's worship (*ishrak fi'l 'ibada*), giving examples illustrating each type. Thus, belief in intercession is cited as an example of association of others with God's power. A host of popular practices, such as prostration before a tomb, going on pilgrimage to a holy person's tomb and making food offerings in honor of the deceased, and the like are cited as examples of the third kind of *shirk*. However, Sayyid Ahmad did not condemn sufism *per se*, only its perceived excesses. In addition, he also promoted practices which he deemed Islamic, such as the remarriage of widows (the upper-caste Hindu prohibition on the remarriage of widows had no scriptural sanction in the Qur'an). He even helped to bring about the remarriage of women he knew.

The second phase of Sayyid Ahmad's career was overtly political, for he decided in the early 1820s to wage a jihad against the new non-Muslim rulers of India (first the Sikhs in Panjab, then the British). He and his associates planned for it carefully. First Sayyid Ahmad went on the pilgrimage to Mecca, gathering followers along the way from his hometown in Rae Bareli to Calcutta, where a number of them boarded a ship for the long journey. After his arrival in Arabia, he had his followers swear to follow him in the jihad to come. The model in these and other activities was the Prophet, who had led *his* followers to victory against the pagan Meccans from their base in Medina many centuries before. The oath of loyalty had a double significance: at once a spiritual tie between master and disciple (and a promise to abide by certain principles of behavior which distinguished the devotee from the larger society around him), it was also a political act, presaging the coming jihad. His followers regarded him as the *mujaddid* (Renewer) of the new (thirteenth) Islamic century. As we shall see in subsequent chapters, the Ahl-e Sunnat movement disputed this claim.

After his return to India in 1823, Sayyid Ahmad toured the north for two years, organizing and making preparations. He proceeded in a westerly direction, intending to wage jihad from what is today Afghanistan. The shari'a stipulates (following the Prophet's example) that jihad be waged from a Muslim-ruled territory adjacent to a non-Muslim one. Accordingly, the target of the jihad movement was the Panjab, then ruled by the Sikh leader Ranjit Singh rather than the British. In 1831, after a series of military successes, Sayyid Ahmad was killed along with six hundred others as a result of skirmishes with local Afghans who resented the reforms (and taxes) sought to be imposed on them. Leaderless, the movement lingered on for many years in northwestern India but finally petered out in the 1860s.

The Fara'izi Movement

A very different Islamic reform movement, that of the Fara'izis in Bengal, unfolded during the 1820s through to the 1860s. The name derives from the word *farz* (Arabic *fard*; plural *fara'iz* or *fara'id*), or duties of Islam. The leader of this movement was Haji Shari'at Ullah (d. 1840), who returned to Bengal in 1821 after living in the Hijaz in western Arabia for many years. Dismayed by what he saw as the laxity of practice among Bengali weavers and peasants, he preached renewed commitment to the duties of Islam (daily prayer, the Ramadan fast, and the pilgrimage, among other things). Shari'at Ullah also believed that sufism should be limited to the few, for its esoteric teachings were likely to be misunderstood by ordinary believers. His teachings have been compared to those of the Wahhabis, whose ideas were familiar to Shari'at Ullah from his long stay in Arabia.

Rural Bengal at this time was in the midst of a severe economic depression brought about by the Permanent Settlement of 1793, which changed landholding patterns and rendered many peasants landless. The introduction of British factory-made cloth at low prices was also driving Indian weavers out of business and forcing them on to the land. These circumstances help us understand the anti-British aspects of the movement, for Shari'at Ullah ruled that in the absence of functioning qazis and given the non-implementation of shari'a law, Bengal was *dar ul-harb* (as some interpreted Delhi to have become after its occupation by the British in 1803), and that the congregational noontime prayer on Fridays was therefore not permissible. For him the suspension of religious law in lands under British control meant that the normal rules of conduct in other spheres of life no longer applied either. Under the leadership of his son, Dudhu Miyan, Fara'izis were urged to refuse to pay British land taxes. They also boycotted the British courts, settling their differences themselves. The movement was highly successful in forging a sense of unity and self-help among poor Bengali Muslims for a while. However, British reprisals, and the lack of strong leadership after Dudhu Miyan's death in the 1860s led to the movement's decline (Metcalf, 1982: 68–70; Ahmad Khan, 1965).

The Deobandi 'Ulama

In 1867, a new seminary (madrasa) called the Dar al-'Ulum was founded in the small town of Deoband, about eighty miles north of Delhi. It was a new kind of madrasa:

> Its founders, emulating the British bureaucratic style for educational institutions, ... acquired classrooms and a central library. It was run by a professional staff, and its students were admitted for a fixed course of study and required to take examinations for which prizes were awarded at a yearly convocation. Gradually an informal system of affiliated colleges emerged. ...The school was, in fact, so unusual that the annual printed report, itself an innovation, made continuing efforts to explain the organization of the novel system. (Metcalf, 1982: 93–94)

While this may sound fairly unremarkable to the modern reader, it has to be seen in the context of madrasa education at the time. Traditional madrasas consisted of a building attached to a mosque. The students did not have separate classrooms or libraries, and they studied individual texts taught one-to-one, or in a small group, by a single teacher. The texts taught depended on the capacity of the student. When the student had mastered the texts, he received a certificate (*sanad*) from his teacher and could go on to study more advanced books if he so wished from the same or a different teacher. There were no examinations.

The funding of the madrasa at Deoband was different as well. It was financed by private contributions from the residents of Deoband and other well-wishers, not by an endowment (*waqf*), as was customary. Nor was it supported by the patronage of princely courts (as was the Madrasa-i 'Aliyya at Rampur, for instance).

Intellectually, the 'ulama at Deoband had much the same perspective as the Madrasa-i Rahimiyya in Delhi and Shah 'Abd ul-'Aziz (d. 1824). Two 'ulama who were central to the school's founding and early years were Maulanas Muhammad Qasim Nanautawi (1833–79) and Rashid Ahmad Gangohi (1829–1905). Muhammad Qasim's family had a long-standing relationship with the 'ulama of Delhi, as did Rashid Ahmad's. Both were of the reformist tradition; they were critical of the rituals customarily performed at saints' tombs, lavish weddings and feasts, and the payment of interest on loans, for instance. They were also ambivalent about rituals associated with the death anniversaries ('urs) of sufi saints, discouraging but not completely condemning them. On the other hand, they were punctilious about observing the ritual obligations of prayer, fasting, and performance of the pilgrimage. They also sought to encourage widow remarriage. "The follower was expected to abandon suspect customs, to fulfill all religious obligations, and to submit himself to guidance in all aspects of life" (Metcalf, 1982: 76–79, 151).

The fact that the Deobandis were reformist does not mean that they were opposed to sufism – on the contrary, both Qasim Nanautawi and Rashid Ahmad were disciples of the famous Haji Imdadullah – but it did mean that they disapproved of what they considered sufi excesses. The curriculum they taught sought to be comprehensive: they "taught all the Islamic sciences and ... represent[ed] all the Sufi orders. They said that in this they followed Shah Waliyu'llah. [However, unlike him, they] emphasized reform of custom, not intellectual synthesis" (Metcalf, 1982: 140).

For the Deobandi 'ulama, as for those of the Ahl-e Sunnat movement, the writing of fatawa was an important means of disseminating the message. Although the subjects of these legal judgments varied widely, for the most part they steered clear of politics. They addressed questions related to sufism, the proper performance of ritual prayer, fasting, pilgrimage, and relations with other groups, both Muslim and non-Muslim.

Zaman adds to the picture painted by Metcalf by giving an interesting example of the approach to problems thrown up by British rule in the late nineteenth and early twentieth centuries, such as the lack of qadis (judges of Islamic law) in British Indian courts. The judgments of the 'ulama were not enforceable in court. For instance, without a qadi it now became impossible to have marriages annulled. As a result, women began to declare themselves apostates from Islam, since apostasy automatically terminated a marriage. In the 1930s, Maulana Ashraf 'Ali Thanawi (d. 1943), a famous Deobandi scholar ('alim), tried to solve this problem by arguing that apostasy had no effect on the marriage contract, while at the same time proposing both that the conditions under which marriages could be dissolved should be made less stringent and that in the absence of a qadi, 'ulama or other "righteous Muslims" acting together could dissolve a marriage in his stead. These ideas were accepted by the political party, Jamiyyat al-'Ulama-e Hind, which had been founded after World War I and which was dominated by Deobandi 'ulama, and it became the basis for the Dissolution of Muslim Marriages Act of 1939 in British India. As Zaman points out, however, although this solved the problem related to apostasy and made it easier to dissolve a bad marriage, it put no pressure on the British to appoint qadis in British Indian courts.

The Ahl-e Hadith

The movement known as the Ahl-e Hadith ("people of the [prophetic] hadith") derives from the fact that the 'ulama in this group advocated reliance on the Qur'an and hadith for guidance on matters of ritual and behavior. They denied the legitimacy of the four Sunni law schools (Hanafi, Shafi'i, Hanbali, and Maliki) that had emerged within some three hundred years of the death of the Prophet and which had long reached so dominant a position that one could not be a Sunni without affiliation to one of them. Their rejection of the judgments of the law schools and insistence that each believer decide on an issue for him- or herself based on what the Qur'an and hadith have to say about it presupposed a high level of literacy and familiarity with Arabic which the 'ulama were normally the only ones to possess; this made it highly elitist. This was a reflection, perhaps, of their class status, for the leadership of the Ahl-e Hadith belonged to the well-born, people who had been employed by the Mughal court but had since fallen on hard times.

Two additional features distinguished the Ahl-e Hadith from other Sunni Muslims. The first was a ritual matter: they favored a certain manner of prayer that set them apart from everyone else. The second was more important, namely that they condemned all forms of sufism, not just specific aspects of sufi practice after the fashion of the Deobandis. They opposed the veneration of saints and pilgrimages to their tombs. In fact, they also opposed the practice of visiting the Prophet's tomb in Medina. Because of this and their condemnation of the four law schools, many Muslims compared them to the Wahhabis of Arabia. Like the Arabian Wahhabis, they read and admired the works of Ibn Taimiyya (d. 1328), even translating his works into Urdu.

The Ahl-e Hadith, however, claimed that they were intellectual descendants of the eighteenth-century scholar Shah Wali Ullah of Delhi. Shah Wali Ullah had, indeed, spoken of the importance of hadith scholarship, and of the precedence of hadith over the judgments of the law schools in cases of conflict between them. And unlike the Ahl-e Hadith, who "denied the legitimacy of ... the four major law schools" (Metcalf, 1982: 270), at least for the educated elite, the Wahhabis followed the judgments of Hanbali scholars. Unlike Shah Wali Ullah, who had been eclectic in his use of the legal tradition, the

Ahl-e Hadith preferred a narrow interpretation of the Qur'an and hadith.

Relations between the Ahl-e Hadith and the other Sunni Muslim reform movements were tense, leading on several occasions to lawsuits which the British were forced to arbitrate. Their relations with the British were also uneasy. The British suspected them of sedition until 1871, when they concluded the so-called Wahhabi trials conducted against the jihadists who had continued to fight the British in Afghanistan and along the northwestern border, following Sayyid Ahmad Barelwi's lead. Thereafter relations between them improved.

In terms of their theological positions on the Sunni law schools and sufism, the Ahl-e Hadith was perhaps the furthest from the Ahl-e Sunnat of all the movements considered here.

The Nadwat al-'Ulama

The Nadwat al-'Ulama ("Council of 'Ulama," known as Nadwa, for short) was founded in the 1890s in the hope of bringing Sunni and Shi'i 'ulama together on a single platform, despite their differences of opinion. It was hoped that, thus united, the Nadwa would be able to present to the British the views of its members on issues they cared about. Annual meetings were planned at which all members would convene and decide on future action. As originally conceived, its membership was to have consisted not only of Sunni and Shi'i 'ulama, but also of wealthy and powerful patrons such as Muslim "princes, government servants, traders, and lawyers" (Metcalf, 1982: 345). It was also conceived as an all-India body, not a local one. It actively sought British recognition of its school, the Dar al-'Ulum, founded in 1898. After some hesitation, the British agreed to patronize secular learning at the school, contributed land for the fine building subsequently built in Lucknow, and in 1908 laid the foundation stone.

The school curriculum was a source of considerable debate and discord from the very outset. Some felt that English should be taught alongside Arabic and other subjects since it would allow the Nadwa to refute Western religion and culture all the more effectively. Although two of its early leaders, Sayyid Muhammad 'Ali Mongiri and Maulana Shibli Numani, supported English as a subject, the 'ulama opposed it, and the idea soon had to be given up. The opposition stemmed from fear that in the long run the introduction of English would lead to the secularization of the curriculum.

Another goal of the new school was madrasa reform. In order to

> infus[e] the ranks of the 'ulama with fresh vigor, and … broaden the scope of their activities and their role in the Muslim community … it was deemed imperative to reform the prevalent styles of learning. …The Nadwa's proposed curriculum sought to produce religious scholars capable of providing guidance and leadership to the community in a wide range of spheres: in law and theology, in *adab* (belles lettres), in philosophy, and in "matters of the world." (Zaman, 2002: 69)

The founders hoped that all Indian madrasas would follow its lead and adopt the curriculum that they proposed to put together. They wanted to impart a "useful" education – by which they meant one that would create "a new generation of 'ulama fit to lead the Muslim community." The study of "exegesis [of the Qur'an], hadith, history, and Arabic literature" was to be emphasized, while that of logic and philosophy – the hallmark of the Dars-i Nizami syllabus they were trying to reform – was downplayed (Zaman, 2002: 71–72). If this sounds counterintuitive, it has to be remembered that the Dars-i Nizami syllabus had been designed in the eighteenth century. The Nadwa considered it outdated and in need of revision. Exegesis of the Qur'an and hadith, on the other hand, required the student to study the sources at first hand, while the study of Arabic literature and history were intended to broaden the student's knowledge of the Arab world more generally.

In practice, it was hard to implement these changes, for the authority of the 'ulama ultimately rested on their mastery of the very texts that the Nadwa was trying to replace. (Indeed, Zaman points out that the authority of these texts had, if anything, increased during the colonial period.) The Nadwa's proposal to do away not only with many of these texts, but also with the discursive practices of the madrasa curriculum – in other words, with the whole system by which religious authority was acquired and demonstrated – required the 'ulama to distance themselves from their tradition of learning, rather than embrace it. Another hurdle was the difficulty of getting the 'ulama to put aside their differences. The challenge the Nadwa thus took on was enormous, and in the end the attempt failed.

The Nadwa continues to flourish today, but its curriculum follows that of the Dars-i Nizami syllabus.

Sayyid Ahmad Khan and MAO College, Aligarh

Sayyid Ahmad Khan (d. 1898) was not a religious scholar but an official in the judicial department of the British Indian government until his retirement in 1877, and the college he founded in 1875 had a very different purpose from those discussed above. He is an important figure in the history of South Asian nationalism, particularly in Pakistan, where he is seen as the nineteenth-century "founder" of the idea of a separate homeland for South Asian Muslims. When the Indian National Congress was founded in 1885, Sayyid Ahmad spoke out against the idea of an Indian nation that might be democratic when it became independent, as he believed this would be detrimental to Muslim interests, and founded an organization of his own, the Muhammadan Educational Congress (later renamed the Muhammadan Educational Conference). Shortly thereafter, the British honored him with a knighthood for his services to the empire in the aftermath of the Revolt of 1857, particularly the role he played in fostering mutual understanding between the British and the Indian Muslim community, and he became Sir Sayyid.

Sayyid Ahmad Khan was a rationalist. His reformist ideas were in the tradition of Shah Wali Ullah, and were also similar to those of Muhammad Isma'il, the author of the *Taqwiyat al-Iman*, particularly in his disapproval of what he saw as accretions to Islamic belief and practice and different forms of associationism (*shirk*). He believed that Islam was a rational religion, one that was in full accord with human nature:

> I have determined the following principle for discerning the truth of the religions, and also for testing the truth of Islam, i.e., is the religion in question in correspondence with human nature or not, with the human nature that has been created into man or exists in man. And I have become certain that Islam is in correspondence with that nature. (Quoted in Troll, 1978: 317)

And further:

> I hold for certain that God has created us and sent us his guidance. This guidance corresponds fully to our natural constitution, to our nature. ... It would be highly irrational to maintain that God's work [the natural world, including humankind] and God's word [the revelation of the Qur'an] are different and unrelated to one another. All beings, including man, are God's work and religion is His word; the two cannot be in conflict. ... So I formulated that "Islam is nature and nature is Islam." (Quoted in Troll, 1978: 317)

This formulation led some 'ulama, the Ahl-e Sunnat among them, to allege that Sayyid Ahmad Khan worshiped nature rather than God, an allegation he vehemently denied.

In keeping with his modernist, rationalist thinking Sayyid Ahmad Khan denied the possibility of miracles, interpreting the miracles surrounding the Prophet as later fabrications. He also interpreted belief in angels metaphorically rather than literally, as a quality possessed by prophets. Thus, the angel Gabriel "stands for the ... inherent possession of prophethood in the Prophet himself and thus stands for the cause of revelation" (Troll, 1978: 181). He was also critical of much of the hadith literature, dismissing it as being inauthentic. Like the Ahl-e Hadith, he denied the legitimacy of the four Sunni law schools, looking to the Qur'an and the example of the Prophet for guidance. On the power of personal prayer (dua) to change one's ultimate fate, he believed that God "is pleased with such prayer and accepts it as He accepts any other form of service. ... Performance of this prayer brings about in man's heart patience and firmness" (Troll, 1978: 182). But he held that it did not change one's predetermined destiny. The concept of intercession and mediation between man and God were thus also denied.

Sayyid Ahmad Khan's reformist ideas were intimately connected with the political context of late nineteenth-century British India. He came from a family which had been associated with Mughal rule, and he keenly felt the loss of that rule. In his view, Muslims had lost out to the British because they had failed to keep up with the scientific progress of the West and had allowed their practice of the faith to lapse as well. Judging that British rule over India was there to stay for the foreseeable future, he set out on the one hand to cultivate good relations with the British and on the other to encourage Muslims to acquire the new linguistic and scientific skills necessary to succeed in the new era.

In the educational realm, Sayyid Ahmad Khan's modernist, progressive vision expressed itself in the Muhammadan Anglo-Oriental (MAO) College, founded in Aligarh in 1875. The college was modeled on Oxford and Cambridge (he had spent two years, 1869–70, in Britain, studying everything from factories to schools). Not only would the curriculum offer an array of Western subjects (the natural sciences, mathematics, literature, and so on), but it would also be residential. Over the years, as David Lelyveld (1978) eloquently demonstrates, the school fostered a strong sense of belonging – even brother-hood – among the students, many of whom had come from outside the immediate geographical area. Sayyid Ahmad Khan's goal of training a generation of Muslims who would become part of the new government structure was also partially real-ized, to the extent that three-quarters of school graduates got government positions. But there could be no sense of equality between the British and Aligarh's Muslims: "however skilled in Western culture some Indians might become, the pall of arro-gant racism, inherent in the colonial situation, meant that full acceptance of Indians as equals never happened" (Metcalf, 1982: 334).

Sayyid Ahmad Khan had to concede defeat on the religious front as well. So controversial a figure was he on account of his reformist ideas that the Muslims of Aligarh and elsewhere were initially reluctant to support his new institution. The British stepped in not only with funds but in many cases with profes-sors as well. Sayyid Ahmad did his best to reassure Muslim parents that their children would not be taught radical ideas by hiring some of his fiercest critics as professors in the religious studies department. Consequently the program of religious education at MAO College, while reformist in the Deobandi sense, appears to have been uncontroversial.

In sum, Aligarh's MAO College was a Western-style institu-tion, unlike the Dar al-'Ulum at Deoband and that of the same name started by the Nadwat al-'Ulama in Lucknow in the 1890s. It shared with them a sense that Islamic education needed reform in order to be meaningful in the late nineteenth century. Unlike the Deobandi madrasa, both the Nadwa and Sayyid Ahmad Khan also aspired to some form of political association with the British. In the early twentieth century, MAO College – which was recognized as a university and renamed Aligarh Muslim University in 1920 – fulfilled its promise by becoming the training ground for several prominent Indian Muslim nationalists.

The Ahmadi Movement

The Ahmadi movement, which was highly controversial, was founded by Mirza Ghulam Ahmad (d. 1908), in 1889. Ghulam Ahmad was born in the village of Qadiyan, Panjab, in the 1830s, to a family that had prospered during Mughal times but had lost much of its wealth during Sikh rule. He credited the British with an improvement in his family's fortunes, and in later years was noticeably pro-British in his politics. His education was traditional (study of the Qur'an, Arabic, and other subjects), but acquired at home, not at a madrasa.

Unlike most of the other Muslim movements discussed in this book, the Ahmadis can date the beginning of their movement precisely, for in March 1889 Ghulam Ahmad held a ceremony of sufi initiation (bay'a) at which he accepted his first disciples in the city of Ludhiana, Panjab. From 1891 onward, the group held annual meetings each December "to enable every Ahmadi to increase his religious knowledge by listening to speeches, ... to strengthen the fraternal bonds between the members, and to make plans for missionary activity in Europe and in America" (Friedmann, 1989: 5). The initial activities of the movement revolved around public oral debates with

Hindus (the Arya Samaj) about miracles and eternal salvation, with Christians about the death of Jesus Christ and Christ's divinity, and with other Muslims (the Ahl-e Hadith), also about Jesus Christ. Ghulam Ahmad was also a prolific writer of books and articles in Urdu, Arabic, and Persian, and in 1902 began an English monthly periodical, *The Review of Religions*, which has continued to be published ever since. The third significant thrust of the movement has been a missionary one, with emphasis particularly on growth in Britain.

The disagreements between the Ahmadiyya and other Sunni Muslims in South Asia are mainly over Ghulam Ahmad's claims to religious authority. He believed he was the "*mujaddid*, renewer (of religion) at the beginning of the fourteenth century of Islam; *muhaddath*, a person frequently spoken to by Allah or one of His angels; and *mahdi*, 'the rightly guided one, the messiah,' expected by the Islamic tradition to appear at the end of days" (Friedmann, 1989: 49). Of the three claims made here, the second, that of being spoken to by Allah, was particularly controversial, as the rank of *muhaddath* is considered to be only slightly below that of prophethood and implies direct communication with God. No Sunni reformer had ever claimed it before. By contrast, the claim to the status of Mahdi is relatively common in Sunni history, and several claimants appeared in the eighteenth and nineteenth centuries, associated with anticolonial jihad movements against British or French rule. It was not, however, as a militant Mahdi that Ghulam Ahmad cast himself. On the contrary, he denied not only the obligatory nature, but also the very legitimacy of jihad in the sense of armed confrontation, an extraordinarily bold heretical move only partly explained in terms of his positive attitude to British rule. In his view, jihad was to be interpreted as the peaceful attempt to spread the faith through conversion.

Ghulam Ahmad was fierce in his denunciation of the Indian

'ulama, who in his view had allowed Islam to fall into a sorry state:

> Like leaders of other revivalist and messianic movements in Islam, Ghulam Ahmad was convinced that Islamic religion, Islamic society, and the position of Islam vis-à-vis other faiths sank in his times to unprecedented depths. Corruption, blameworthy innovations (*bida'*), tomb worship (*qabr parasti*), worship of Sufi shaykhs (*pir parasti*), and even polytheism became rampant. The Islamic way of life was replaced with drinking, gambling, prostitution, and internal strife. The Qur'an was abandoned, and (non-Islamic) philosophy became the people's *qibla* [guide]. (Friedmann, 1989: 105)

More specifically, Ghulam Ahmad accused the 'ulama of failing to stem the tide of Christian influence in India. Ghulam Ahmad propounded a number of anti-Christian arguments. In agreement with the Qur'an (4: 157), he maintained that Christ had not died on the cross, but whereas most Muslims believe that he is alive and will return together with the Mahdi, Ghulam Ahmad claimed that he had died at the age of a hundred and twenty and was buried in Srinagar, the capital of Kashmir. For Ghulam Ahmad, belief in the death of Jesus was important in light of the Christian missionaries' denunciation of the Prophet Muhammad as a dead prophet, in contrast to Jesus Christ who, they said, was alive in heaven and would one day return (as the Sunnis agreed). In Ghulam Ahmad's depiction of the second coming, he, Ghulam Ahmad, would be the messiah, not Jesus Christ. "By claiming that Jesus died a natural death, Ghulam Ahmad tried to deprive Christianity of the all-important crucifixion of its founder. In doing this he was following classical Muslim tradition. By claiming affinity with Jesus, he went one step further: he tried to deprive Christianity of Jesus himself" (Friedmann, 1989: 118).

Two further theological ideas need to be understood in this brief summary, namely, Ghulam Ahmad's ideas about prophecy and his claim to be a "shadowy" (*zilli*) prophet himself. As Friedmann makes clear, these ideas – and indeed other aspects of Ghulam Ahmad's thought – are based on sufi concepts traceable to Ibn 'Arabi (d. 1240). Ibn 'Arabi believed that the total cessation of prophecy after the death of the Prophet Muhammad would have left the Muslim community utterly bereft. This was impossible in his view, so he postulated that prophecy had continued in a new form. There were two different types of prophecy, he said, the legislative, which is superior and which had ceased on the death of the Prophet, and the non-legislative, which is given to sufis of extraordinary caliber and insight and which he claimed for himself. Friedmann sums up the difference, in Ghulam Ahmad's view, between the Prophet and himself as follows:

> while it is true that no law-giving prophet can appear after
> Muhammad, prophetic perfections are continuously
> bestowed upon his most accomplished followers, such as
> Ghulam Ahmad, to whom Allah speaks and reveals his secrets.
> However, since Ghulam Ahmad attained this position only by
> his faithful following of Muhammad, his prophethood does
> not infringe upon Muhammad's status as the seal of the
> prophets. (Friedmann, 1995: 56)

Furthermore, after Muhammad's mission had been completed, Muslims were the only ones favored with direct communication from God by having people among them who were *muhaddath*. This proved their superiority over Christianity.

A few years after Ghulam Ahmad's death in 1908, the movement split into two factions, subsequently known as the Qadiyanis and the Lahoris (after the places where they have their headquarters; Qadiyan is now in India, Lahore in Pakistan). The Qadiyanis, led by Ghulam Ahmad's son, were more numerous and supported Ghulam Ahmad's prophetic claim, while the Lahoris watered it down, rejecting his claim to prophethood and only accepting him as a Renewer (*mujaddid*) rather than a prophet. (In the 1970s and 1980s, the Ahmadis of both factions were declared non-Muslims in Pakistan by a constitutional amendment and other legislative means.)

3

AHMAD RIZA KHAN: LIFE
OF A MUSLIM SCHOLAR

A hmad Riza Khan was born in Bareilly, in the western
United Provinces, in 1856, just a year before the great
Indian Revolt. A story is told about his grandfather, Maulana
Riza 'Ali Khan (1809–65/66), relating to the British resump-
tion of control over Bareilly after the Revolt had been put down
in that town:

> After the tumult of 1857, the British tightened the reins of
> power and committed atrocities toward the people, and
> everybody went about feeling scared. Important people left
> their houses and went back to their villages. But Maulana Riza
> 'Ali Khan continued to live in his house as before, and would
> go to the mosque five times a day to say his prayers in
> congregation. One day some Englishmen passed by the
> mosque, and decided to see if there was anyone inside so they
> could catch hold of them and beat them up. They went inside
> and looked around but didn't see anyone. Yet the Maulana was
> there at the time. Allah had made them blind, so that they
> would be unable to see him. ... [When] he came out of the
> mosque, they were still watching out for people, but no one
> saw him. (Bihari, 1938: 5)

Bihari goes on to quote the Qur'anic verse, "And We shall raise
a barrier in front of them and a barrier behind them, and cover

them over so that they will not be able to see" (36: 9, Ahmed 'Ali translation).

The story is interesting at many levels. It casts Maulana Riza 'Ali as a fierce opponent of the British who put his trust in God instead of fleeing and who was so holy and so good that God protected him, blinding the enemy to his presence. This miracle, for so it was described (*karamat*), was a sign of his eminence as a sufi (mystic). The title of Maulana before his name shows that he was also a religious scholar (*faqih*). Or, to put it another way, he didn't just practice his faith by meticulously adhering to the Law (shari'a), he also lived it and breathed it in his inner being.

Ahmad Riza Khan's family had not always been associated with religious learning. His ancestors were Pathans who had probably migrated from Qandahar (in present-day Afghanistan) in the seventeenth century, joining Mughal service as soldiers and administrators. One family member eventually settled down in Bareilly, where he was awarded a land grant by the Mughal ruler. There followed a brief interlude in Awadh, when Ahmad Riza Khan's great-grandfather served the nawab in Lucknow, probably in the late 1700s, when Mughal power was in decline and Awadh in the ascendant. The nawab is said to have given Hafiz Kazim 'Ali Khan, Ahmad Riza's great-grandfather, two revenue-free properties. These properties were in the family's possession until 1954 (Hasnain Riza Khan, 1986: 40–41).

We know that Hafiz Kazim 'Ali later returned to Bareilly, for that is where his son Riza 'Ali (Ahmad Riza's grandfather) grew up. It was Riza 'Ali who made the break from soldiering and state administration to become a scholar and sufi. In the early nineteenth century, at a time when Muslim states all over India were bowing to British power, the opportunities for a soldier who sought a Muslim patron were diminishing rapidly. Riza 'Ali was educated at Tonk, the only Muslim state in central India (where, as mentioned in the previous chapter, Sayyid Ahmad had been a soldier in the ruler's army in the 1820s). After completing his study of the Dars-i Nizami syllabus there by the age of twenty-three, he returned to Bareilly and made his reputation as a scholar.

Ahmad Riza's father, Naqi 'Ali Khan (1831–80), carried on the scholarly tradition begun by his father, while also looking after the family properties. By this time the family owned several villages in the adjoining districts of Bareilly and Badayun. The Revolt of 1857 did not affect the family significantly, though some property in Rampur was lost in its aftermath because of failure to find the title deeds and prove ownership to the British. Relations with the British appear to have been indirect but cordial. Ahmad Riza's nephew Hasnain Riza owned a printing press which later published many of Ahmad Riza's writings. Hasnain Riza reportedly collected certain fees from the police tribunal for the British, acted as arbitrator between Muslims in the town, and mediated between them and the British on occasion. He did not, however, work for the British in an official capacity.

The family also had close ties with officials in Rampur state, which, as noted in chapter 1, retained its independence under a Muslim nawab throughout the period of British rule. Thus, for instance, Ahmad Riza's father-in-law was an employee at the Rampur Post Office, and attended the nawab's court (Hasnain Riza Khan, 1986: 152). Rampur's nawabs had been Shi'is since the 1840s – all but one, that is: Kalb 'Ali Khan (r. 1865–87) who was a Sunni.

RAMPUR STATE

As noted earlier (pp. 6–7), Rampur state was founded by Faizullah Khan in the 1770s by treaty with Warren Hastings, then the Governor of Bengal. It was all that was left to the Rohillas after the absorption of Rohilkhand by the up-and-coming state of Awadh to the east. Having acquired a little state of his own, Faizullah Khan put down his arms and devoted the remaining years of his life to developing Rampur as a center of Muslim cultural life and sought to attract writers, poets, and other men of literary or scholarly talent to his court. There is some evidence that he founded the Raza Library, which is in operation to this day, home to a large collection of valuable manuscripts in Arabic, Persian, and Urdu.

Awadh became increasingly indebted to the East India Company over the course of the early nineteenth century, and was finally forced to cede power to the Company altogether in 1856. The Rampur court then rose as an alternative source of patronage to which people would travel in search of employment. "Mulla Hasan [of Farangi Mahall] went from Lucknow to Shahjahanpur, and thence to Rampur via Delhi; Mawlana 'Abd 'Ali Bahr al-'Ulum (1731–1810) from Lucknow to Shahjahanpur, to Rampur, to Buhar in Bengal and finally to Madras" (Robinson, 2001: 23). The 'ulama of Farangi Mahall, it should be noted, were Sunni by persuasion. The Rampur court, which became Shi'i in the 1840s, was hospitable to both Sunnis and Shi'is.

The court welcomed a number of poets, most famously, in the nineteenth century, Mirza Ghalib (d. 1869), who taught poetry to Rampur's nawab, Yusuf 'Ali Khan (r. 1855–65). Yusuf 'Ali was himself a poet. From 1859, he began to send Ghalib a regular monthly grant for correcting his poetry and writing occasional panegyrics on important state occasions. Contrary to custom (and Yusuf 'Ali's preference), Ghalib was permitted to live in Delhi, making only occasional visits to the Rampur court. Ghalib, like many of his contemporaries, wrote not only in Persian – the language of choice for the educated elites of all communities, Muslim as well as Hindu, throughout the eighteenth and the first half of the nineteenth centuries – but also in Urdu, which rapidly began to replace Persian in the second half of the nineteenth century. Thus, Ahmad Riza Khan's writings, which I will examine in later chapters, were almost entirely in Urdu.

The madrasa at Rampur known as 'Aliyya also attracted well-known 'ulama from other parts of north India. Among them were Maulanas Fazl-e Haqq Khairabadi (d. 1861) and 'Abd ul-Haqq Khairabadi (d. 1899), both specialists in the rational sciences (*ma'qulat*). It was founded in the eighteenth century with endowment (*waqf*) funds from two villages, and enjoyed state patronage under the nawabs. However, it never achieved the status of other madrasas in the country, such as Farangi Mahall in Lucknow or the Madrasa-i Rahimiyya in Delhi, where Shah Wali Ullah taught in the eighteenth century. Rampur's Raza Library, on the other hand, was an institution of great renown. For seven years, from 1896 to 1903, it was managed by the famous Indian nationalist leader, Hakim Ajmal Khan (1863–1927), who expanded the library's holdings on medicine (*tibb*), enabling it to become one of the best in the country. A new library building was also constructed at the end of the nineteenth century.

AHMAD RIZA'S EDUCATION AND SCHOLARLY TRAINING

Ahmad Riza's most important teacher was his father. He studied the Dars-i Nizami syllabus under his direction, and imbibed from him the rationalist tradition. The pattern of a student studying specific books under a single teacher, whether in an institution such as a madrasa (seminary) or at the teacher's home, was traditional throughout the Muslim world. At the end of the period of study, the teacher would give the pupil a certificate (*sanad*) stating that the student had studied certain books under his direction (including glosses and commentaries thereon) and giving him permission (*ijaza*) to teach these in turn. Thereafter, if he so wished, the student could continue his studies under another teacher, with whom he would remain until he had obtained another certificate testifying to competence in another set of books. Chains of transmission of authority – recorded in writing at the end of a period of study – were thus established between individual teachers and their students, for each teacher received the authority to teach from the one who had taught him. Over time, these chains of authority linked a vast network of 'ulama in different parts of the country (for an example of such a chain of ma'qulat scholars, see Robinson 2001: 52–53).

Not surprisingly, in view of the strong ties between teachers and their students, the intellectual positions taken by the former often stamped themselves indelibly on the minds of the latter. So it was with Ahmad Riza Khan. His father's stand on a number of theological issues in the mid-nineteenth century later also became his own.

SCHOLARLY IMPRINT OF HIS FATHER

One of the well-known debates of the early nineteenth century dealt with God's omnipotence. Some 'ulama argued that God had the power, should He so wish, to create another prophet like Muhammad. Thus, Muhammad Isma'il, author of the *Taqwiyat al-Iman* (Strengthening the Faith), had written in the 1820s:

> in a twinkling, solely by pronouncing the word "Be!" [God could], if he like[d], create crores [tens of millions] of apostles, saints, genii, and angels, of similar ranks with Gabriel and Muhammad, or produce a total subversion of the whole universe, and supply its place with new creations. (Mir Shahamat 'Ali, tr. (modified), 1852: 339)

This statement – known as *imkan-e nazir*, the possibility of an equal (of the Prophet) – was made in the context of *tawhid*, as an illustration of God's power. It was strongly opposed by Maulana Fazl-e Haqq Khairabadi, whose presence at the Madrasa 'Aliyya at Rampur and association with the rationalist position in 'ulama circles were mentioned earlier. Maulana Fazl-e Haqq – taking a position known as *imtina'-e nazir*, or impossibility of an equal – argued that even God could not produce another prophet like the Prophet Muhammad.

A generation later, in the 1850s and 1860s the two views were expressed again, both verbally and in print, with Naqi 'Ali Khan, Ahmad Riza's father, echoing Maulana Fazl-e Haqq Khairabadi's position. In the 1890s, Ahmad Riza Khan himself wrote a responsum (fatwa) in which the focus of discussion was no longer on God's transcendental power but rather on the uniqueness of the Prophet. Arguing that it was impossible for anyone ever to equal the Prophet (not only in this world but in any of the six levels of the earth believed to exist apart from this one), he declared that to maintain otherwise amounted to denial of the finality of his prophethood and thus to *kufr*, unbelief. Although the terms of debate had shifted from a discussion of God's powers to Muhammad's prophethood, Ahmad Riza's stance on this issue, as on others as well, was clearly influenced by his father.

EXEMPLARY STORIES

Ahmad Riza's biographer, Zafar ud-Din Bihari, records a number of stories about Ahmad Riza's spiritual and intellectual accomplishments as a child. Each of them illustrates a distinctive aspect of the way his followers came to see him in later life. Thus, when learning the Arabic alphabet from his grandfather, Ahmad Riza is said to have instinctively understood the deeper significance of the letter "la" – a composite letter with which the attestation of faith (the *kalima* or *shahada*, lit. "witness") begins. He grasped not only its outward meaning, that related to the Oneness of God, but also its inner, gnostic meaning, communicated to him by his grandfather. This story is significant in light of the fact that Ahmad Riza went on to become both an 'alim or scholar of Islamic law, and a sufi or mystic seeker of God.

Other stories claim that at four, Ahmad Riza had memorized the entire Qur'an by heart, and at six he addressed a gathering of worshipers at the mosque from the pulpit on the occasion of the Prophet's birthday (an annual celebration at which he addressed large crowds from the mosque in later years). When studying the Dars-i Nizami from his father he showed that he had outstripped him in knowledge by answering a criticism noted by him on the margins. His father was very happy to see this and embraced him. And when he was fourteen – much younger than most scholars in a comparable situation – and had finished his studies in both the rational (ma'qulat) and copied (manqulat) sciences, his father entrusted him with a great responsibility, that of writing fatawa (Bihari, 1938: 11, 31–33). This was to be the hallmark of his later career as a scholar. The number of fatawa he wrote from then until his death in 1921 was said to be in the thousands.

Ahmad Riza's superiority of intellect to other 'ulama far older than him is also illustrated in several stories. Shortly after his marriage, when he was about twenty, he gave an opinion that contradicted that of a famous scholar at the Rampur court, Maulana Irshad Hussain Rampuri. The nawab noticed this and upon enquiry discovered that Ahmad Riza was the son-in-law of one of his courtiers. So he asked to meet him (Bihari, 1938: 135). Accordingly, Ahmad Riza Khan came to court. Impressed by both his youth and his erudition, the nawab suggested that Ahmad Riza would profit by studying under the famous Maulana 'Abd ul-Haqq Khairabadi, who had a reputation as a scholar of logic and who attended the Rampur court. Ahmad Riza replied that if his father gave his permission, he would be happy to stay in Rampur for a few days and study with 'Abd ul-Haqq. Just then 'Abd ul-Haqq himself came into the room. The story continues:

> Maulana 'Abd ul-Haqq believed that there were only two and a half 'ulama in the world: one, Maulana Bahr ul-'Ulum ['Abd al-'Ali of Farangi Mahall, d. 1810–11], the second, his father [Fazl-e Haqq Khairabadi, d. 1861], and the last half, himself. How could he tolerate this young boy being called an 'alim? He asked Ahmad Riza: Which is the most advanced book you have read in logic?
>
> Ahmad Riza answered: *Qazi mubarak.*
>
> He then asked: Have you read *Sharah tahzib*?
>
> Ahmad Riza Khan, hearing the derision in his voice, asked: Oh, do you teach *Sharah tahzib* after *Qazi mubarak* over here?
>
> ['Abd ul-Haqq decided to try a different approach. He asked:] What are you working on right now?
>
> Ahmad Riza: Teaching, writing of fatawa, and writing.
>
> 'Abd ul-Haqq: In what field do you write?
>
> Ahmad Riza: Legal questions (*masa'il*), religious sciences (*diniyat*), and rebuttal of Wahhabis (*radd-e wahhabiyya*).
>
> 'Abd ul-Haqq: Rebuttal of Wahhabis? [A discussion about the best authority in this field of disputation followed, at the end of which 'Abd ul-Haqq fell silent.] (Bihari, 1938: 33–34)

The tone of the exchange leaves the reader in no doubt as to the winner. Ahmad Riza Khan had defeated 'Abd ul-Haqq Khairabadi, who belonged to an eminent family of 'ulama in the *ma'qulat* tradition, with links to Farangi Mahall. Robinson goes so far as to say that the Farangi Mahalli family's "impact in northern India ... was intensified by the development of a powerful offshoot, another great school specializing in ma'qulat scholarship, that of Khayrabad in western Awadh, whose notable scholars [included] Fazl-e Haqq Khairabadi" (Robinson, 2001: 67). Given that Ahmad Riza's family also adhered to the tradition of *ma'qulat* studies rather than the hadith scholarship emphasized by the Shah Wali Ullah family in Delhi, there was no philosophical difference between the two men. Moreover, Ahmad Riza's youth and his own family's relative obscurity in the world of 'ulama scholarship (which only went back two generations) compared to 'Abd ul-Haqq's at this time, would lead one to expect him to be deferential to the older man. Instead, the conversation as reported by Zafar ud-Din Bihari indicates that Ahmad Riza had already mastered the works of logic (standard texts of the Dars-i Nizami syllabus) that the nawab of Rampur had suggested he study under 'Abd ul-Haqq. The only person who ever corrected any of Ahmad Riza Khan's writings, Bihari reports, was his father, Naqi 'Ali Khan.

Apparently Ahmad Riza Khan took a personal dislike to 'Abd ul-Haqq Khairabadi, for we are told that on another occasion when Ahmad Riza was traveling to Khairabad with a revered friend of the family, who was planning to visit 'Abd ul-Haqq Khairabadi, Ahmad Riza refused to accompany him, saying that 'Abd ul-Haqq was in the habit of saying things "detrimental to the glory (*shan*) of the ... 'ulama", and that he would therefore prefer to visit someone else (Bihari, 1938: 176).

The fact that Ahmad Riza's visit to the nawab's court was occasioned by his writing an opinion that contradicted Maulana Irshad Hussain Rampuri's is also part of this pattern. If the exchange with Maulana 'Abd ul-Haqq tells the reader about the depth of his learning and the range of his scholarship (I will examine what he meant by "rebutting Wahhabis" in a subsequent chapter), his contradiction of Maulana Irshad Hussain is intended to show that he had an independent mind, was a skillful logician, and had outstripped his elders early on in his career. The spirit of competition demonstrated here was also to characterize the claims and counterclaims made by rival Muslim movements in the later nineteenth century.

SUFI DISCIPLESHIP TO SHAH AL-E RASUL OF MAREHRA

If the responsibility for writing fatawa at age fourteen at the end of his Dars-i Nizami studies marked a watershed in Ahmad Riza's life, so too did his discipleship to Sayyid Shah Al-e Rasul in 1877, when he was twenty-one. Shah Al-e Rasul was in his eighties at the time and died two years later, so the tie between them was not close – for Ahmad Riza had not spent time with him prior to his discipleship, not even the customary forty-day period (*chilla*) of waiting and training. Shortly before his death, however, Shah Al-e Rasul entrusted Ahmad Riza's spiritual development to his grandson, Shah Abu'l Husain Ahmad, known as Nuri Miyan (1839–1906), who was Ahmad Riza's senior by about fifteen years, and the relationship between the two men did become close.

THE IMPORTANCE OF DREAMS

Ahmad Riza's biography indicates the importance of the tie between Shah Al-e Rasul and Ahmad Riza by reference to dreams. Thus it is recorded that before his journey to Marehra with his father, Ahmad Riza experienced a period of painful spiritual longing. His grandfather appeared to him in a dream and assured him that he would soon be relieved of his pain. The prophecy was fulfilled when Maulana 'Abd ul-Qadir Badayuni came to their house and suggested that both father and son affiliate themselves to Shah Al-e Rasul. Shah Al-e Rasul was also awaiting his arrival, for he already knew (we are told) that this new disciple would be the gift he could present to God after his death, when God would ask him what he had brought Him from this world (Hasnain Riza Khan, 1986: 55–56). Because he was already so well advanced spiritually, the forty-day waiting period had not been necessary.

SAYYIDS OF THE QADIRI ORDER OF SUFIS

The decision as to whom Ahmad Riza and his father should bind themselves (for they did so together) in this all-important relationship was probably dictated in part by Shah Al-e Rasul's genealogical history. The Barkatiyya family of Marehra to which Shah Al-e Rasul belonged were Sayyids, or descendants of the Prophet through his daughter Fatima and son-in-law 'Ali. His very name "Al-e Rasul," meaning "[the] family of the Prophet," indicates as much. Other males in the family had similar names. Shah Al-e Rasul's younger brother, for example, was called Awlad-e Rasul, or "children of the Prophet." Women in the family were often named Fatima or a compound thereof, such as Khairiyat Fatima, "Fatima's well-being." Although such names were not limited to Sayyid families, in this case they were indicative of such status.

The Barkatiyya Sayyids had migrated to India, via Iraq and Ghazni (in present-day Afghanistan), in the thirteenth century. They had settled down in Marehra, a small country town (qasba) about a hundred and twenty miles southeast of Delhi, in the seventeenth century, after an earlier period of residence in Bilgram, western Awadh. The Mughals had awarded religious families such as the Barkatiyya Sayyids revenue-free (mu'afi or madad-e ma'ash) lands to support them. The family name probably referred to their illustrious seventeenth-century ancestor, Sayyid Barkat Ullah (1660–1729), who founded the hospice (khanqah) around which later generations of the family lived and grew up. In time, their settlement came to be known as "Basti Pirzadagan" (Qadiri, c. 1927).

The sufi affiliation of the Barkatiyya Sayyids was with the Qadiri order, one of the three major sufi orders in India since the eighteenth century (the others are the Chishti and the Naqshbandi). The Qadiri order traces its origins to 'Abd al-Qadir Jilani Baghdadi (d. 1166), and has been popular in South Asia since the fifteenth century. I take up the significance of this sufi affiliation to Ahmad Riza in the next chapter.

GOING ON PILGRIMAGE, 1878

Shortly after Ahmad Riza became Shah Al-e Rasul's disciple in the ritual known as bai'a, he and his father undertook another important journey, namely, the pilgrimage to Mecca. By performing this ritual, Ahmad Riza was fulfilling one of the so-called "pillars" of Islam, a necessary step before he could assume his role as the leader and Renewer of his community. In this sense, he was undertaking a rite of passage, a transformative event which allowed him to return to Bareilly with greater authority.

Mecca and Medina, the two holiest cities for Muslims, were under Ottoman control at this time. Mecca is the center of the Muslim pilgrimage because it houses the sanctuary which Abraham is believed to have built with his son Ishmael in antiquity and also because it is the city in which Muhammad was born. By the nineteenth century it was first and foremost as the Prophet's birthplace that it was revered. Medina, the city where Muhammad lived in the second phase of his career and where he is buried, is not a part of the pilgrimage. But because he is buried there, many Muslims making the pilgrimage visit it too. Ahmad Riza and his father, not surprisingly, went to both places.

While Ahmad Riza was in Mecca he received recognition from 'ulama in high positions of authority. Sayyid Ahmad Dahlan, the mufti of the Shafi'i law school, gave him a certificate (*sanad*) in several fields of knowledge – hadith (the traditions of the Prophet), exegesis of the Qur'an (*tafsir*), jurisprudence (*fiqh*), and principles of jurisprudence (*usul-e fiqh*). The other scholar to do so was the mufti of the Hanafi school of law. Although Ahmad Riza had not studied under these scholars formally they authorized him to teach in the fields they had specified and to cite their names when doing so.

Equally important, though in a different way, was his encounter with Husain bin Saleh, the Shafi'i imam. The latter noticed him one day during the evening prayer and took him aside. We are told that he held "his forehead for a long time, saying at length that he saw Allah's light in it. He then gave him a new name, Zia ud-Din Ahmad, and a certificate in the six collections of hadith, as well as one in the Qadiri order, signing it with his own hand" (Rahman 'Ali, 1961: 99). This encounter emphasized the spiritual (sufi) rather than the scholarly sources of Ahmad Riza's authority. So too did another – Medinan – experience, a dream in which Ahmad Riza was assured that he was absolved of all his sins. As most Muslims believe that this assurance is granted to very few, this vision can be read as a claim to leadership of the Ahl-e Sunnat movement in coming years.

AHMAD RIZA AS *MUJADDID*

Ahmad Riza's proclamation as the *mujaddid* of the fourteenth Islamic century occurred in unusual circumstances and in an unusual manner. Throughout the 1890s the Ahl-e Sunnat had been busy organizing meetings opposing the Nadwat al-'Ulama. Ahmad Riza had played an active part in this opposition movement, writing some two hundred fatawa on this issue alone. Starting in 1897, the Ahl-e Sunnat also published a monthly journal (*Tuhfa-e Hanafiyya*, the Hanafi Gift) from

Patna, Bihar, which brought together anti-Nadwa articles, poems, and news reports about the annual meetings. It was in print until about 1910.

Ahmad Riza's stature was heightened when one of his fatawa was published in 1900 with the approval and certification of sixteen 'ulama from Mecca and seven from Medina. In October of that year the annual meeting of the Ahl-e Sunnat 'ulama took place in Patna, during which time a new madrasa, the Madrasa Hanafiyya, was formally opened. The Nadwa was holding its own annual meeting in a different part of town. In fact the Ahl-e Sunnat appears to have deliberately chosen to hold its meeting in the same place and at the same time as the Nadwa, in order the better to undercut its message.

It was during the week-long meetings that occurred at Patna that one of the 'ulama present referred to Ahmad Riza in his sermon as the "*mujaddid* of the present century." According to Zafar ud-Din Bihari, all those present seconded the idea, and later thousands of others, including several 'ulama from the Haramain (Mecca and Medina) did so as well. As he writes, there was thus consensus among the 'ulama of the Ahl-e Sunnat on the question. Zafar ud-Din adds that Ahmad Riza fulfilled the requirements of a *mujaddid*, namely, that he (it could not be a woman) be a Sunni Muslim of sound belief, endowed with knowledge of all the Islamic "sciences and skills," the "most famous among the celebrated of his age," defending the faith without fear of "innovators" who would criticize him, and also, according to Zafar ud-Din, a profound sufi. He also had to satisfy the technical requirement that he be well known when one century ended and the other began (or, as Bihari puts it, at the end of the century in which he was born and the beginning of the century in which he was to die). The thirteenth Islamic century had ended on 11 November 1882, and Ahmad Riza had indeed begun to establish a reputation among the 'ulama of north India by then. The fact that 'ulama in Mecca and Medina

were ready to append their names to his commentary on the
Prophet's knowledge of the unseen (see below) was taken by
his followers as confirmation that he was indeed the *mujaddid* of
the fourteenth Islamic century.

FATWA WRITING

Ahmad Riza's scholarly reputation rested primarily on his writing of fatawa, a responsibility entrusted to him by his father when
he was fourteen and carried out until his death in 1921. A fatwa
is written in answer to a question asked by a Muslim man or
woman to a mufti, a scholar of Islamic law, about a legal or moral
problem, such as an inheritance dispute, a debate about vari-
ations in the prayer ritual, or questions of faith and belief. The
legal questions are not usually of the type posed to lawyers in the
West, for the law in which the mufti is an expert is religious law.
The nearest equivalent in the West to a fatwa is rather the answers
to the questions posed to "the Ethicist" in the *New York Times*
Sunday Magazine. In a Muslim city, there are hundreds of
"ethicists," all willing to answer questions. They are the religious
scholars, known as muftis when they act as authors of fatawa.

To qualify as a mufti, a scholar needs to have expert knowledge of sources of the law – the Qur'an, the sunna (the
example of the Prophet), the consensus of the community
(*ijma*), and analogical reasoning (*qiyas*) – as well as familiarity
with the legal tradition of the school (*madhhab*) to which he
himself and the questioner belong. If no direct answer could be
found in the sources, a person endowed with such knowledge
was qualified to apply his judgment (*ijtihad*) to the question at
hand. The latitude permitted to a mufti – or that he permitted
himself – in interpreting the sources has varied considerably
throughout Muslim history. For many centuries *ijtihad* had
been downplayed, and following one's school of law (*taqlid*)

had been the norm. This was also the case in colonial India. But regardless of the mufti's theoretical stand on *ijtihad*, the activity had never ceased in practice, since new problems and questions constantly needed answers. The mufti's answer, while considered authoritative (on account of his knowledge), did not have the force of law.

The question-and-answer format of a fatwa is also worth noting. Some hold it to go back to the Prophet himself, on those occasions when he acted in his own capacity when asked a question: "It is reported, for example, that [a believer] asked the Prophet, 'O Messenger of God, is the pilgrimage to be performed every year or only once?' He replied, 'Only once, and whoever does it more than once, that is an [especially meritorious] act'" (Masud, Messick, and Powers, 1996: 6). Such reports are recorded in the hadith literature, which complements the Qur'an as a secondary source. In later generations, the activity of the mufti was seen as a continuation of the Prophet's example. Thus the fourteenth-century scholar al-Shatibi wrote that "the mufti stands before the Muslim community in the same place as the Prophet stood" (Masud, Messick, and Powers, 1996: 8).

Because the work of writing fatawa was "religious" in nature – in other words, it was a means of guidance and benefit to other Muslims – muftis were forbidden to take bribes or gifts of any kind from the person who had asked the question. Even private muftis were expected to render their judgments for free (muftis who worked for the state received salaries, like the qadis in Islamic courts). Whether all did so is unlikely. In some cases, the problem of compensation was solved by the creation of pious endowments (*awkaf*) specifically for muftis and teachers.

In colonial India, as noted in previous chapters, the loss of state power and the lack of qadis in British Indian courts increased the need for muftis, as they were the sole authority left to guide the community. The latter half of the nineteenth century also saw a rapid increase in communications networks and new and inexpensive print technologies that allowed 'ulama such as Ahmad Riza to reach a wider group of people and forge a network of relationships beyond the immediate local area. This created competition for followers, especially as different reform movements made their appearance, so that the activity of writing and publishing fatawa became highly competitive. They were a way of reaching the hearts and minds of Sunni Muslims throughout the subcontinent, since they dealt with practical issues rather than academic problems of an erudite nature.

HIDDEN CUES IN A FATWA, OR WHAT A FATWA MAY NOT TELL US

Fatawa vary from the very short and simple to the long and complex, depending on their intended audience – those written for ordinary believers tend to be simple, straight-forward, and without citation of sources, while those written by scholars for scholars were naturally likely to be complex. However, even when simple in form, a fatwa often contains hidden cues about the scholar's point of view. An example from a Deobandi fatwa about the pilgrimage, written by Maulana Rashid Ahmad Gangohi (d. 1905) in the 1890s, is instructive:

> Query: What of a person who goes to Noble Mecca on hajj and does not go to Medina the Radiant, thinking, "To go to Noble Medina is not a required duty, but rather a worthy act. Moreover, why should I needlessly ... risk ... property and life [in view of the marauding tribes along the way] ... and [spend] a great deal of money?" ... Is such a person sinful or not?

Answer: Not to go to Medina because of such apprehension is a mark of lack of love for the Pride of the World [the Prophet Muhammad], on whom be peace. No one abandons a worldly task out of such apprehension, so why abandon this pilgrimage? … Certainly, to go is not obligatory. [But] some people, at any rate, think this pilgrimage is a greater source of reward and blessing than lifting the hands in prayer and saying "amin" out loud. Do not give up going out of fear of controversy or concern for your reputation. … Even if not a sinner, this person lacks faith in his basic nature. (Metcalf, 1996: 184)

At first sight the fatwa seems only to be answering a simple question, namely, what the mufti thinks of a nonobligatory ritual act, that of paying homage to the Prophet by visiting his grave at Medina while performing the pilgrimage to Mecca (the latter being incumbent upon all adult Muslims, men and women, to perform once in their lifetimes). But on second reading you notice that it engages in polemics against the Ahl-e Hadith.

Since Medina is not far from Mecca (about 270 miles north), many Muslims make the journey there either before or after the pilgrimage itself. But the reply contains several clues that tell us that the question and answer were directed against the Ahl-e Hadith. The practice of "lifting the hands in prayer and saying 'amin' out loud" was specific to the Ahl-e Hadith and distinguished them from other Sunni Muslims in South Asia. It was also the Ahl-e Hadith who "opposed pilgrimage (*ziyarat*) to the Prophet's tomb in Medina, as they opposed pilgrimage to all tombs," sharing the orientation of the Wahhabis who "had gone so far as to destroy the tomb of the Prophet" in the early nineteenth century (Metcalf, 1996: 186–187).

Now let us look at a very different case, also from Deoband. Masud's (1996) study of two Deobandi fatawa shows how the 'ulama sometimes initiated a process of change in the shari'a (by applying their independent reasoning), but used the citation of respected medieval sources to present their judgment as an exercise in submission to authority (*taqlid*), that is, the authority of their particular school of law, which in British India was (and is) overwhelmingly Hanafi. By comparing two fatawa by Maulana Ashraf 'Ali Thanawi (d. 1943) on whether the apostasy of a Muslim woman annulled her marriage, Masud shows that Thanawi changed his position between 1913, the date of his first fatwa, and 1931, when he revised his opinion. In 1913, he had ruled that apostasy did result in annulment, whereas in 1931, applying Maliki law (thus having recourse to legal opinion in another school, or *talfiq*), he argued that "apostasy did not annul the marriage contract and could not be used as a legal device [to terminate the marriage]" (Masud, 1996: 193–203; cf. p. 37, on the legal issue).

The fatwa is a clear case of the application of *ijtihad*, but is not presented as such. Had the argument been seen as an instance of *ijtihad* being exercised by a single mufti rather than one which had the weight of traditional jurisprudential authority behind it, it might not have been accepted. As this instance shows, *ijtihad* – far from being something the mufti could be proud of engaging in – had to be wrapped up in the guise of *taqlid*.

This case – dealing with apostasy and the difficulty Muslim women experienced in initiating a divorce – is clearly more complex than the first. The 1931 fatwa (the revised one) was published as a book of over two hundred pages. Its publication led to a political effort for marriage reform by the national party representing Deobandi and other 'ulama, the Jamiyyat al-'Ulama-e Hind, and in 1939 resulted in the enactment of national legislation in British India to facilitate the dissolution of Muslim marriage on specific legal grounds.

AHMAD RIZA'S FATAWA

Like the other Muslim movements of the late 1800s, the Ahl-e Sunnat movement established a Dar al-Ifta, a "house for issuing fatawa." Unlike the other movements, however, that of the Ahl-e Sunnat was attached to Ahmad Riza's house rather than to the school established in 1904. It was from here that, assisted by his closest and ablest students, he responded to the questions that came in daily from all over the country.

Zafar ud-Din Bihari, Ahmad Riza's disciple and biographer, relates that every evening Ahmad Riza would set aside some time to meet people at his home. The day's mail would sometimes be opened and read out loud. Depending on the nature of the question, Ahmad Riza would either answer it himself or pass it on to one of his students to do so. Thus, if it dealt with sufism (*tasawwuf*), was particularly complex, or had not come up before, he would answer it himself. Subjects deemed less difficult were handled by a small group of students. He worked in the privacy of his personal library or in his family living quarters (*zenana khana*), and took pride in answering every question as quickly as possible. Regarding it as a religious (*shar'i*) duty, he was offended when someone offered him payment for his fatwa. So devoted was he to the task of responding (*istifta*), wrote Zafar ud-Din, that he did so even when he was sick. We are told that on one remarkable occasion he was seen dictating twenty-nine fatawa to four scribes while sick in bed: while one scribe wrote down the answer to one question, he dictated the answer to the second one to another, and so on, until all twenty-nine questions had been answered (Bihari, 1938: 36–37, 68).

It was by writing down and copying fatawa dictated by Ahmad Riza that his students learned his style of fatwa-writing. Once they had mastered the skill, Ahmad Riza was able gradually to entrust some of the work to them. He considered his student Amjad 'Ali A'zami to be the most skilled, and asked other students to learn from him.

Many – though by no means all – of Ahmad Riza's fatawa were published in a twelve-volume collection known as the

Fatawa-e Rizwiyya, some at the Hasani Press owned by his brother. Only two appear to have been published during his lifetime. Publication of the others did not begin until the 1950s, and was still ongoing in the 1980s. The process was begun by Maulana Mustafa Riza Khan (d. 1981), Ahmad Riza's younger son. Perhaps the lack of funds held back further publication. Unfortunately, when publication was finally resumed it was found that many of the handwritten fatawa were damaged, and laborious effort was required to assemble the later volumes. Nonetheless, most of them were published. A different problem arose when a printer kept delaying publication on one pretext or another until the editors caught on to the fact that he had Deobandi views!

Some fatawa discuss a range of issues related to the question but nevertheless distinct from it, especially when they are long and complex. Ahmad Riza tended to expand, rather than restrict the range. So too did the Deobandis in the same period. As Metcalf says, "Any categorization of the topics covered in [Rashid Ahmad Gangohi's] pronouncements is necessarily crude, for a single fatwa could often illustrate at once a variety of issues concerning belief, practice, jurisprudential principles, and attitudes toward other religious groups" (Metcalf, 1982: 148). In a fatwa responding to the question as to whether a Muslim who had become an Ahmadi was an apostate, Ahmad Riza raised issues relating not only to apostasy and marriage but also to the nature of prophecy.

Ahmad Riza's opinions were always forcefully expressed. He was decisive in his judgments, giving clear guidance to his followers on right and wrong and backing up his opinions by citation of an array of scholarly writings that added to his religious authority. At a time when so many different points of view were being expressed, one imagines that the ordinary believer would have found this note of certainty reassuring.

TWO FATAWA WRITTEN DURING AHMAD RIZA'S SECOND PILGRIMAGE TO MECCA

In 1905–6, Ahmad Riza went to Mecca and Medina for the second time. In 1906, Mecca was a place where diverse opinions flourished. The Wahhabi movement (consisting of an alliance between the followers of Muhammad ibn 'Abd al-Wahhab and the Saudi family) was based in Najd in central and eastern Arabia. In the Hijaz (as coastal northwestern Arabia is known), however, power was in the hands of Sharif 'Ali (r. 1905–8) of Mecca. Although technically the Sharif (also known as Amir) was an appointee of the Ottomans – the Hijaz being a province of the Ottoman empire – in fact the amir exercised autonomous control. Sharif 'Ali died in 1908, whereupon Sharif Husayn – memorably portrayed in the film *Lawrence of Arabia* for his part in leading the Arab Revolt against the Ottomans – came to power.

Ahmad Riza's views found a receptive audience among some Meccan 'ulama who disliked the Wahhabi perspective. By this time he was a well-known Indian scholar, one who had been in correspondence with the 'ulama of the Hijaz during the 1890s when he had sought confirmation for his fatawa in opposition to the Nadwa. Two Meccan 'ulama now asked for his opinion on the status of paper money. In response he wrote a fatwa entitled *Kafl al-Faqih al-Fahim fi Ahkam Qirtas al-Darahim* (Guarantee of the Discerning Jurist on Duties relating to Paper Money). One scholar reportedly stated, "Although he was a Hindi [an Indian], his light was shining in Mecca" (*Malfuzat*, vol. 2, p. 17). There were other marks of respect: confirmation of his opinion on a ritual related to the pilgrimage (despite a contrary opinion by some Meccan scholars) and visits to his home. Bearing in mind that only a segment of the 'ulama was involved, we might even say that relations between center and periphery, Mecca and India, had been reversed during Ahmad Riza's three-month stay.

Ahmad Riza wrote three fatawa while in Mecca. While the first is the one on paper money, the second, *Al-Dawlat al-Makkiyya bi'l Maddat al-Ghaybiyya* (The Meccan Reign on That Which Is Hidden), deals with the Prophet, particularly his "knowledge of the unseen" (*'ilm-e ghaib*), which had been an object of debate between Ahmad Riza and the Deobandi 'ulama for some time. (The third fatwa, *Husam al-Haramayn 'ala Manhar al-Kufr wa'l Mayn* [The Sword of the Haramayn at the Throat of Unbelief and Falsehood], is discussed in the next chapter.)

Ahmad Riza made two related arguments in *Al-Dawlat al-Makkiyya*. The first was that God's knowledge is distinct from that of the Prophet. As he wrote:

> One is the *masdar* or source, from where knowledge emanates, and the other is dependent upon it. In the first case, knowledge is *zati*, that is it is complete and independent in itself. ... In the second case, it is *'ata'i*, that is "gifted" by an outside source. *Zati* knowledge is exclusively Allah's. ... The second kind is peculiar to Allah's creatures. It is not for Allah. (*Al-Dawla al-Makkiyya*, 15, 17, 19)

Having made this fundamental distinction between God's knowledge and the Prophet's, Ahmad Riza then proceeded at great length (the fatwa is approximately two hundred pages long) to lay out the scope of the Prophet's knowledge of the unseen. He began by saying that some knowledge of the unseen is possessed even by ordinary human beings: Muslims believe in the resurrection of the dead, heaven and hell, and other unseen things, as commanded by God. The knowledge possessed by prophets was of course much greater than that of ordinary people, and although it was but a drop in the ocean compared to what God knows, it was itself "like an ocean beyond counting, for the prophets know, and can see, everything from the First Day until the Last Day, all that has been and all that will be" (*Al-Dawlat al-Makkiyya*, 57, 59).

As for the Prophet, his knowledge kept growing as the Qur'an was revealed to him over a twenty-two-year period (610–32 CE). Thus, Qur'anic passages that refer to his lack of knowledge about something refer to a time when knowledge of the particular matter still had not been revealed, and were abrogated by later verses on that subject. By the end of his life, however, God had told him about

> the tumult of the resurrection (hashr o nashr), the accounting, and the reward and punishment. So much so that he will see everyone arriving at their proper places [at the end of times], whether heaven or hell, or whatever else God may tell him. Undoubtedly, the Prophet knows this much, thanks to God, and God alone knows how much else besides. When He has given his beloved [Muhammad] so much, then it is apparent that knowledge of everything in the past and the future, which is recorded in the Tablet (lawh-e mahfuz) is but a part of his knowledge as a whole. (Al-Dawlat al-Makkiyya, 77)

The Prophet also knew what was going on inside people's minds: "He knows the movement and glance of the eyelid, the fears and intentions of the heart, and whatever else exists" (Al-Dawlat al-Makkiyya, 90).

And, most controversially (for the Deobandis, among others, denied this), the Prophet had knowledge of the five things referred to in Qur'an 31: 34:

> Only God has the knowledge of the Hour.
> He sends rain from the heavens,
> and knows what is in the mothers' wombs.
> No one knows what he will do on the morrow;
> no one knows in what land he will die.
> Surely God knows and is cognisant.
> (31: 34, Ahmed 'Ali trans.)

Ahmad Riza argued that apart from the resurrection, the other four things – knowledge of when it would rain, of the sex of a yet unborn child, of what one would earn on the morrow, and of the land where one would die – were not all that significant in themselves. In fact, they were rather minor in scale of importance compared to knowledge of the attributes of God, heaven and hell, and the like. (In fact, Ahmad Riza argued, knowledge of these five things had been given not only to the Prophet, but also to Shaikh 'Abd al-Qadir Jilani, the *qutb* or "pivot" at the head of the invisible hierarchy of saints on whom the government of the world depends.) The reason God had singled out these five things for mention in the Qur'an was that the soothsayers (*kahin*s) of early seventh-century Arabia – the age of the Prophet, when the Qur'an was revealed – believed they could predict such things. God wanted them to know that these things were "hidden" (*al-ghayb*) and that none could know them but He and those He favored. The Prophet had been favored with this knowledge (including the hour of the resurrection) but had been commanded not to reveal it.

Ahmad Riza cited two Qur'anic verses in defense of his views. They were 3: 179, "nor will God reveal the secrets of the Unknown. He chooses (for this) from His apostles whom He will", and 72: 26–27, "He is the knower of the Unknown, and He does not divulge His secret to any one other than an apostle He has chosen" (Ahmed 'Ali trans.).

In keeping with the sufi dimensions of Ahl-e Sunnat belief and practice (discussed in the next chapter), Ahmad Riza also held a number of related beliefs about the Prophet, some of which are found in Shi'ism: that he was God's beloved for whom God had created the world, that Muhammad had been created from Allah's light and therefore did not have a shadow, and, most importantly, that he mediated between God and the Muslim believer in the here and now – one did not have to wait for the last day and the resurrection for such mediation to occur. Ahmad Riza's views about the Prophet's knowledge of the unseen were in keeping with his overall perception of the

Prophet as one who was uniquely endowed by God. Also note-
worthy in this regard is the hierarchy of levels of knowledge
laid out in the above fatwa: after God, Muhammad's knowledge
was greatest, then followed the knowledge of various
prophets, that of the 'ulama and sufi shaikhs and pirs (Shaikh
'Abd al-Qadir Jilani foremost among these), and finally, that of
ordinary believers.

In 1911, Ahmad Riza's translation of the Qur'an, entitled
Kanz al-Iman fi Tarjuma al-Qur'an (Treasure of Faith relating to a
Translation of the Quran), was published in Muradabad, a
north Indian city where some of his followers were based.
Although an English translation was subsequently published by
the Islamic World Mission in Britain, it has yet to receive scholarly attention.

POLITICAL ISSUES IN THE EARLY TEENS AND TWENTIES

In the years leading up to World War I the Indian nationalist
movement united behind the British Crown by sending troops
all over the world to fight on behalf of the British, but with high
hopes that after the war was over the process of self-rule would
be speeded up. Into this mix were added fears on the part of the
Muslim leadership that they might not fare too well in democratic elections in a Hindu-dominated India, and that steps
needed to be taken to safeguard Indian Muslim interests. This
led a small group of Muslim leaders to form the All-India
Muslim League in 1906.

The 'ulama had to decide whether or not they should take a
political stand as well, and if so, whether they should throw
their support behind the Indian National Congress, which was
the dominant nationalist party, or the Muslim League, or

whether they should form a party – or parties – of their own. And if they did form their own party, should they join with Congress in anti-British agitation, or act independently? As may be imagined, there were many different opinions among them, expressed once again in fatawa, commentaries, and other scholarly writings, not to mention oral debates and speeches made during Friday prayers. Ahmad Riza's opinion that there was no *religious* justification for Indian Muslims taking an anti-British stand was challenged by 'ulama from other movements, who accused him of being pro-British.

During the prewar years a number of Indian Muslims had begun to organize around an international issue, that of helping the Ottoman caliph, whose empire was in danger of complete dismemberment by the Allies after the war. This pan-Islamic movement was supported by Indian Muslim leaders such as Abu'l Kalam Azad (1888–1958), who owned and contributed regularly to the influential Urdu journal *Al-Hilal*, and Maulana 'Abd ul-Bari Farangi Mahalli (1878–1926), who was involved in efforts to raise money for Turkish relief from India. In 1913, 'Abd ul-Bari began an association called Society of the Servants of the Ka'ba (Anjuman-e Khuddam-e Ka'ba). Ahmad Riza's support was sought, but he refused – not because he was unsympathetic to the plight of the Turks or because he did not want to protect the Ka'ba, but because he objected to the composition of the Anjuman. Because it strove to be an inclusive body, welcoming all Muslims, whether Shi'a, Ahl-e Hadith, modernist, or other, Ahmad Riza refused to be associated with it. He did so on grounds similar to those he had expressed against the Nadwa in the 1890s, namely, that he could not support a body which included people he deemed "bad" Muslims (*bad-mazhab*) or those who had "lost their way" (*gumrah*), his terms for the groups mentioned above.

Although he was all in favor of helping the Turks financially, Ahmad Riza believed that given the straitened circumstances of

Indian Muslims there was not much that they could do, and he was critical of what he saw as the wasteful expenditure of resources by politically active 'ulama. In a 1913 fatwa he expressed his sympathy for the plight of the Turkish people, quoting Qur'an 13: 11: "Verily God does not change the state of a people till they change it themselves" (Ahmed 'Ali trans.). After suggesting that both the Turks and the Indian Muslims would ultimately have to depend on their own resources rather than external help, he went on to suggest that if every Muslim donated a month's salary, living for twelve months on eleven months' earnings, they would be able to render the Turkish Muslims substantial help.

In addition, he proposed a fourfold course of action aimed at making the Indian Muslim community economically and polit- ically self-sufficient: first, by boycotting the British Indian courts (as he was to do in 1917) they would save money on stamp duties and legal fees. Secondly, they should buy whatever goods they needed from fellow Muslims, thereby keeping money within the Muslim community (and not allowing them- selves to go into debt to Hindu moneylenders). Thirdly, wealthy Muslims in large cities such as Bombay should open interest-free banks for use by Muslims. And finally, all Indian Muslims should strengthen themselves by acquiring the know- ledge of their faith (Ahmad Riza Khan, 1913).

This is the only fatwa known to me in which Ahmad Riza addressed himself to practical issues rather than religious ones. It is interesting that he concentrated entirely on eco- nomic self-sufficiency, and said nothing about political action. To the end of his life he remained convinced that the Indian Muslim community needed internal reform rather than political independence. His reference to Hindus in this fatwa is also revealing. In his view, political alliances forged with Hindus for the sake of overthrowing the British were mis- placed.

Taking Ahmad Riza's cue, leaders of the Ahl-e Sunnat movement formed their own associations and organizations addressing such issues as helping the Turks, instead of joining nationally
prominent ones such as the Anjuman. In fact, several other
Muslim groups formed associations of this kind in the teens and
twenties of the twentieth century. But fissures began to appear
in the Ahl-e Sunnat movement as a younger generation of
Ahl-e Sunnat 'ulama challenged his apolitical stance. I follow
this development in chapter 5 by studying a debate on a matter
of religious ritual, the call to prayer, which culminated in a
court case in 1917.

Not surprisingly, the politicization of the Muslims was
speeded up by the war. The Khilafat movement, launched in
1919 to preserve the caliphate after the Ottoman defeat in
World War I, was the first national movement in which Hindus
and Muslims struggled side by side against the British in support of a specifically Muslim issue. By this time Mohandas
K. Gandhi (known as Bapu ["father"] to his followers) had
returned to India after many years in South Africa and had
assumed leadership of the Indian National Congress.
Determined to work toward Hindu–Muslim unity, he saw in
the khilafat issue an opportunity to bring the two sides
together. In 1920, the Muslim leadership reciprocated by
urging Indian Muslims to join with the Indian National
Congress in its nationwide Noncooperation movement
(1920–2) to oust the British from India. The Noncooperation
movement involved everything from giving up British honors
(titles bestowed on eminent Indians, for example) to
boycotting British courts and schools and the nonpayment of
taxes.

On the Muslim side of the Khilafat movement were
leaders such as Maulana 'Abd ul-Bari, the 'Ali brothers
(Shaukat 'Ali and Muhammad 'Ali), Maulana Azad, Mufti
Kifayatullah, 'Abd ul-Majid Badayuni (a sufi disciple of

Maulana 'Abd ul-Muqtadir Badayuni), and a number of
Deobandi 'ulama, including Shabbir Ahmad 'Usmani and
Husain Ahmad Madani. In 1919 they had created the first
national political organization of 'ulama, namely, the Jam'iyyat
al-'Ulama-e Hind (Society of the 'Ulama of India). Its goals
were at once pan-Islamic (protection of Arabia, particularly
the holy cities of Mecca and Medina) and national (the
promotion of Muslim Indian interests and pursuit of freedom
from British rule). Deeming the British rulers the greater
enemy, it was willing to cooperate with Hindus on the national
front.

Ahmad Riza, characteristically, opposed the Khilafat movement. Part of his objection related to his insistence that the sultan of Turkey could not claim the title of caliph as he was not
of Quraysh descent (there were other *shar'i* conditions as well,
though this was the most important). The other had to do with
his view that Muslims could not seek the cooperation of *kafirs*
(unbelievers) in the pursuit of a religious (*shar'i*) goal – a clear
indication that he was looking at the Khilafat movement in religious rather than political terms.

HIJRAT MOVEMENT

In the late summer of 1920, Maulana 'Abd ul-Bari launched a
new movement, known as the Hijrat (Emigration) movement.
He issued a fatwa declaring that Muslims should abandon
British-ruled India and migrate to a neighboring Muslim territory. Hoping that they could acquire land in Afghanistan, some
twenty thousand people – most of them Pathans from what is
today the Northwest Frontier Province in Pakistan, but also
peasants from the United Provinces and Sind – sold their pos-
sessions and marched toward Kabul. However, Amir
Amanullah Khan (r. 1919–30) had just come to power in

Afghanistan in the previous year, having launched a jihad against the British (an event known to history as the Third Afghan War) with the help of Afghan religious leaders, to get rid of British control of the country. Although defeated, he had concluded a settlement with the war-weary British that accorded Afghanistan full independence, including control over foreign affairs. Fearing the economic consequences of the influx of so many people, Amanullah closed Afghanistan's frontiers to the emigrants, forcing most of them – now destitute – to go back to their homes.

This was the context for Ahmad Riza's fatwa, published in the Rampur newspaper *Dabdaba-e Sikandari* in October 1920, declaring that India was *dar ul-Islam*, or a land of peace, not *dar ul-harb*, a land of war. In fact the fatwa had originally been written in the 1880s, but it was as relevant as ever. He wrote:

> In Hindustan ... Muslims are free to openly observe the two 'ids, the azan, ... congregational prayer ... which are the signs of the shari'a, without opposition. Also the religious duties, marriage ceremony, fosterage ....There are many such matters among Muslims ... on which ... the British government also finds it necessary to seek fatawa from the 'ulama and act accordingly, whether the rulers be Zoroastrian or Christian. ... In short, there is no doubt that Hindustan is dar al-Islam. (Ahmad Riza Khan, 1888–9)

Despite the anti-British sentiment among Indian Muslims at this time, he continued to insist that the fundamental *shar'i* status of the country had not changed. There was thus no justification for either jihad or hijrat.

A flood of accusations of his pro-British sympathies followed, including an allegation that he had met with the Lieutenant Governor of the United Provinces, Sir James Meston, while in Naini Tal, the hill retreat where he went in the last few years of his life to observe the Ramadan fast. He also had to answer charges of lack of concern for the Turks and the holy cities of Mecca and Medina.

AHMAD RIZA'S POPULARITY AMONG CORE FOLLOWERS

While Ahmad Riza's views on national issues may not have enjoyed widespread support outside the Ahl-e Sunnat movement, he continued to be revered and loved by his core group of followers to the end of his life. An event in 1919 illustrated this clearly. That year, he undertook a long journey by train from Bareilly to Jabalpur, in central India, to perform the *dastar-bandi* (tying of the turban) ceremony (which marks the end of a student's career, akin to a student's graduation ceremonies), for one particular student, Burhan ul-Haqq Jabalpuri (d. 1984). By this time his health was poor, and the journey of about six hundred miles took two days. He was greeted like royalty not only at the Jabalpur station, but at smaller stations along the way. People thronged to kiss and touch his feet, and lined the streets on the way to the station.

Once arrived there, Ahmad Riza was surrounded by well-wishers and distributed lavish presents to all and sundry, not just to his hosts. Zafar ud-Din Bihari writes about everybody's amazement at the money, gold ornaments, and clothes which he had brought as gifts. In return, they gave *nazar*, a token gift given to a sufi pir, and feasts throughout his one-month stay. Bihari also reports that at a series of public meetings people came forward to seek his pardon for sins of omission and commission — some of them minor, such as shaving the beard or dyeing the hair black, both of which he disapproved of. Spiritual matters of deeper import were discussed in private sessions (Bihari, 1938: 56–57).

PASSING ON THE LEADERSHIP

In the years before his death in 1921, Ahmad Riza made a series of decisions about the leadership of the movement in the future. Already in 1915, as reported by the *Dabdaba-e Sikandari*, he had chosen his older son, Hamid Riza Khan (1875–1943), as his sufi successor (*sajjada nishin*). After 1921, Hamid Riza became the head of what came to be known as the Khanqah-e 'Aliyya Rizwiyya, the new sufi order named after Ahmad Riza. Ahmad Riza's younger son, Mustafa Riza Khan (1892–1981), had been active in the Dar al-Ifta during the teens of the twentieth century. In the twenties, he was involved in organizational activities centered on defense of the Arab holy cities and rebuttal of the Arya Samaj. In addition, he was a scholar in his own right and did a great deal to collect and publish his father's works. In the 1930s, he started a second school in Bareilly, which is still functioning today.

In 1921, Ahmad Riza passed on to both his sons (and a nephew) the responsibility for writing fatawa. Responding to a question whether India would ever gain its freedom from the British, and if so how qadis and muftis would be appointed, he told his audience that one day:

> The country will definitely become free of English
> domination. The government of this country will be
> established on a popular basis. But there will be great
> difficulty in appointing a qadi and a mufti on the basis of
> Islamic shari'a law. ... I am today laying the foundation for this
> [process] so that ... no difficulty will be experienced after
> independence. (Rizwi, 1985: 20–21)

He then proceeded to appoint one of his close followers, Amjad 'Ali 'Azami, as the qadi, and two others – Mustafa Riza Khan and Burhan ul-Haqq Jabalpuri – as muftis to assist him. This qadi would be the qadi for all India, he said. The fact that he believed he was choosing an all-India qadi speaks to the way he viewed the Ahl-e Sunnat movement, as part of the worldwide, universal *umma* or community of Sunni Muslims. To his mind its reach and status were pan-Islamic, not merely local. That these arrangements were not in fact realized reflects the reality on the ground, in that the future of the Indian Muslim community was largely determined by people and events far removed from Bareilly. The Ahl-e Sunnat movement, though by no means absent during the momentous events of the 1930s and 1940s in British India, was but a small part of a larger whole.

4

AHMAD RIZA KHAN'S BELIEF SYSTEM AND WORLDVIEW

By the 1880s, Ahmad Riza had begun to establish an identity of his own as a mufti who wrote erudite works, including daily responsa (fatawa) in response to questions from Bareilly Muslims and others in distant places, and as a sufi surrounded by a close group of disciples. His perspective was markedly hierarchical. In the spiritual sphere, what mattered most was "closeness" to God, just as in the scholarly one it had been the amount of knowledge the person had. By both measures, the Prophet came first, followed by the founder of the Qadiri order, and finally the sufi master to whom the individual believer was linked through discipleship.

In his personal life, Ahmad Riza took pains to follow the sunna (the "way") of the Prophet down to the smallest detail. It was because they gave primacy to the Prophet in their lives that Ahmad Riza and his group of followers referred to themselves as the "Ahl-e Sunnat wa Jama'at," or "devotees of the Prophet's practice and the broad community." Ahmad Riza's biographer, Zafar ud-Din Bihari (who was also part of his inner circle of disciples), gives us the following picture of Ahmad Riza:

> He wouldn't put any book on top of a book of *hadith* [traditions of the Prophet]. ... When reading or writing, he would draw his legs together, keeping his knees up. ... He

never stretched his legs out in the direction of the *qibla* [the
direction of prayer in Mecca]. He offered all his daily prayers
in the mosque [not just the Friday noontime prayer, as
required by law] (Bihari, 1938: 28).

Elsewhere, Zafar ud-Din relates that when Ahmad Riza
entered the mosque, he did so with his right foot first, while
upon leaving it, he did so with his left foot. Even within the
mosque, he made sure he stepped up to the *mihrab* (the prayer
niche) with his right foot first (Bihari, 1938: 177).

As should be clear from this, the daily lives of the 'ulama
were governed by strict etiquette (*adab*). Like Ahmad Riza, the
famous 'ulama of Farangi Mahall were always mindful of the
example of the Prophet. Maulana 'Abd ur-Razzaq (1821–89),
for example, "is portrayed as following the Prophet in
almost every possible respect. When he drank water, he did so
in three gulps. When he ate, he did so sparingly. ... And before
he began he always said 'Bi'sm allah'" (Robinson, 2001: 83).
Veneration of the Prophet also caused many 'ulama to be
very respectful of sayyids, descendants of the Prophet: thus,
Maulana 'Inayat Ullah, one of the Farangi Mahall scholars,
"revered the Prophet's family, excusing a sayyid hundreds of
rupees rent he owed for the sake of his ancestor. For the same
reason ... he even went so far as to always use the respectful '*ap*'
rather than the usual '*tum*' when he spoke to the sayyids
amongst his pupils" (Robinson, 2001: 84). Similarly, when
Ahmad Riza discovered that a young man hired as household
help was a sayyid, he forbade everyone in the house to ask him
to do anything, asking that they take care of his needs instead.
Uncomfortable with all the attention, after a while the man left
of his own accord.

Ahmad Riza was not just a strict Sunni in the sense of imita-
tor of the Prophet's conduct, however, but also a sufi of the
Qadiri order.

AHMAD RIZA AS A SUFI

Ahmad Riza became Shah Al-e Rasul's disciple (murid, lit. seeker) in 1877. He seems to have thought of the relationship between master and disciple as unbreakable by the disciple even after the master's death, even though it had not necessarily been close in his lifetime. That at least is how he treated the relationship with his own master, Shah Al-e Rasul, who had died a mere two years after it had been formed. As mentioned already, Shah Al-e Rasul's grandson, Nuri Miyan, took over as Ahmad Riza's spiritual director (though technically they were sufi "brothers" or pir bhai, being disciples of the same pir), and Ahmad Riza continued to pay his respects to his deceased master by commemorating his death every year at his home in Bareilly.

The reason the relationship with the pir was so important, according to Ahmad Riza, was that the pir had a unique insight into his disciple's mental frame of mind, and was always on hand to guide him:

> Sayyid Ahmad Sijilmasi was going somewhere. Suddenly his
> eyes lifted from the ground, and he saw a beautiful woman.
> The glance had been inadvertent [and so no blame attached to
> him]. But then he looked up again. This time he saw his pir
> and teacher (murshid), Sayyid … 'Abd al-'Aziz Dabagh.
> (Malfuzat, vol. 2, p. 45)

On the second occasion the pir had intervened to prevent Sayyid Ahmad Sijilmasi from looking – intentionally, this time – at a woman outside the circle of relatives with whom social intimacy was permitted, and possibly being led astray. Scrupulous Muslims hold the very act of looking at an unrelated woman as sinful because it enables impure thoughts to arise. The Muslim standard is therefore more stringent than the Christian one. For Christians, a sin is committed when the viewer is lustful, but not before: "He who looks at a woman to lust after her has already committed adultery with her in his heart." (Matthew, 5:28). Therefore without a pir's guidance the believer was likely to fall into error. Or, as Ahmad Riza put it elsewhere, "To try [to go through life without a pir] is to embark on a dark road and be mis-led along the way by Satan" (Ahmad Riza Khan, 1901: 9–11).

However, such acts of day-to-day guidance were but a small part of the pir's role in the disciple's life. The most important reason why a person should bind himself to a pir, Ahmad Riza explained, was that pirs are intermediaries between the believer and God in a chain of mediation that reaches from each pir to the one preceding him, all the way to the Prophet and thence to God. Hadith (prophetic traditions) proved, he said, that

> there was a chain of intercession to God beginning with the Prophet interceding with God Himself. At the next level, the sufi masters (masha'ikh) would intercede with the Prophet on behalf of their followers in all situations and circumstances, including the grave (qabr). It would be foolish in the extreme, therefore, not to bind oneself to a pir and thus ensure help in times of need (Ahmad Riza Khan, 1901: 12).

THE PERFECT PIR

The pir, in turn, should conform to four exacting standards: he should be a Sunni Muslim of sound faith (sahih 'aqida), should be a scholar ('alim) qualified to interpret the shari'a, his chain of transmission (silsila) should reach back from him in an unbroken line to the Prophet, and finally, he should lead an exemplary personal life and not be guilty of transgressing the shari'a (Malfuzat, vol. 2, p. 41).

If both master and disciple conformed to these high stand-ards, the disciple would eventually attain a state of complete absorption in his pir, a condition known as fana fi'l shaikh. Nuri Miyan was cast as a perfect illustration of the model of fana:

[Nuri Miyan] loved and respected his [pir, Shah Al-e Rasul]; indeed, he loved everyone who was associated with him, and all the members of his family. He followed his commands, he presented himself before him at his court (*darbar*), he sought his company, he was completely absorbed in him. His face had the same radiance [as Shah Al-e Rasul], his personality had the same stamp (*hal*), he walked with the same gait, when he talked it was in the same tone. His clothes had the same appearance, he dealt with others in the same way. In his devotions and strivings, he followed the same path (*maslak*). The times set apart for rest in the afternoon and sleep at night were times when he went to him particularly, receiving from him guidance in every matter and warning of every danger. (Ghulam Shabbar Qadiri, 1968: 91)

CONTROVERSY ABOUT SUFI INTERCESSION

Belief in the intercession of saintly persons with Allah on behalf of the ordinary believer is controversial in Sunni Islam. Indeed, Muslim reformers have often spoken out against it on the grounds that it is a form of *shirk* or associationism and an accretion to "pure" Islam. Years before, Muhammad Isma'il had written against this very belief (and the practices that arise from it) in his book *Taqwiyat al-Iman*, classifying it as the second of three types of *shirk* (see p. 32). Ahmad Riza, for his part, wrote extensively in favor of such belief, declaring that Muhammad Isma'il's position was contrary to the Qur'an, which gives the prophets the power to intercede with God's "permission" (*izn*), and that it detracted from the Prophet's power, which included the ability to perform miracles.

For Ahmad Riza and the Ahl-e Sunnat movement, which saw sufism as a necessary complement to the law, the intercession of sufi masters and, ultimately, of the Prophet himself was crucial to the relationship between master and disciple, for the living hope that the dead pir (here the ordinary dead are less central than the holy, exalted dead) will intercede for them both in the here and now and when they face Judgment Day. But the living can do something for the dead too: the prayers of the living can increase the dead person's chances of a favorable judgment on Judgment Day through the concept of the transfer of merit (*isal-e sawab*). Haji Imdad Ullah "Muhajir" Makki (1817–99), one of the most famous sufis of the nineteenth century – who belonged to the Chishti order and was respected by 'ulama from a number of rival movements, including the Ahl-e Sunnat – wrote in his book *Faisla-e Haft Mas'ala* (Solution to Seven Problems) that the prayers of the living could help the dead person answer the questions of the two angels Munkar and Nakir correctly when they visited the dead in the grave and thereby ensure his or her ultimate entry into heaven.

The spiritual power or grace (*baraka*, *barkat*) of the pir is believed to be especially strong at his tomb, and indeed to grow over time. As Ewing writes:

> [When a saint dies] his spirit is so powerful and so dominant over the body that the body itself does not die or decay but is merely hidden from the living. The baraka of the saint is not dissipated at the saint's death. It is both transmitted to his successors and remains at his tomb, which becomes a place of pilgrimage for later followers. The *pir* does not actually die in the ordinary sense of the term. He is "hidden," and over time he continues to develop spiritually, so that his baraka increases, as does the importance of his shrine. (Ewing, 1980: 29)

THE THREE CIRCLES OF DISCIPLESHIP

As Ewing points out, a pir's followers fall into three distinct groups which can be visualized as a series of concentric circles.

In the first, outermost circle are the large number of people who come to the pir with everyday problems to be solved, such as curing an illness, ensuring the birth of a son, or answering a request for an amulet to be worn for good luck. Ahmad Riza would pass on all such people to his students, unless their problem had to do with sufism (Bihari, 1938: 68).

Within this outer circle was a smaller "inner circle" of followers in whose training he took great interest. All were known as khalifas (deputies). They were divided into "ordinary" ('amm), the second group, and special (khass), the third group, also the smallest. Some of Ahmad Riza's ordinary khalifas went on, in the 1920s, to become prominent leaders of the Ahl-e Sunnat movement during the Khilafat and Indian nationalist movements. He looked upon them as lieutenants or right-hand men who could be counted upon to debate with an opponent, run a newspaper or school (madrasa), and generally promote the goals of the movement in their hometowns, but did not regard them as spiritual disciples. This relationship, Ahmad Riza said, ceased upon the death of the teacher. His relationship with the khalifa-e khass, on the other hand, was of primarily religious significance and was continuous, not ceasing with the death of the teacher. Those in this small group experienced fana of the pir and saw themselves as tied to their master even after he had died, as described above. Out of this select group the pir would choose one as his successor (sajjada nishin). Ahmad Riza chose his eldest son, Hamid Riza Khan – authorizing him, in November 1915, to continue the chain of sufi discipleship (silsila) named the silsila Rizwiyya (from the "Riza" in his name). The sajjada nishin also bore worldly responsibilities for the maintenance of properties and management of funds (Ahmad Riza Khan, 1901: 14). This ensured the continuity of the sufi master's spiritual and worldly network over time.

SHAIKH 'ABD AL-QADIR JILANI AND THE IMPORTANCE OF THE QADIRI ORDER

Ahmad Riza was affiliated to the Qadiri order (*tariqa*), one of the three major sufi orders in nineteenth-century India (along with the Chishti and Naqshbandi). The Qadiri order was founded in the twelfth century by Shaikh 'Abd al-Qadir, a native of the town of Jilan in Iran, who later became a scholar and preacher in Baghdad. His tomb in Baghdad is visited by pilgrims from all over the Muslim world, particularly from South Asia. To his followers, he is a saint, an intercessor with God, and the occupant of a place of honor in the hierarchy of saints "between this world and the next, between the Creator and the created" (Padwick, 1996: 240). One of his most popular epithets is "Ghaus-e A'zam," the "Greatest Helper." Qadiris regard him as the Qutb, axis or pole of the invisible hierarchy of saints who rule the spiritual universe. This spiritual "government" is as follows:

> Every ghaus has two ministers. The ghaus is known as 'Abd Allah. The minister on the right is called 'Abd al-Rab, and the one on the left is called 'Abd al-Malik. In this [spiritual] world, the minister on the left is superior to the one on the right, unlike in the worldly sultanate. The reason is that this is the sultanate of the heart and the heart is on the left side. Every ghaus [has a special relationship with] the Prophet. (*Malfuzat*, vol. 1, p. 102)

The first ghaus, Ahmad Riza said, was the Prophet. He was followed by the first four caliphs (Abu Bakr, 'Umar, 'Uthman, and 'Ali), each of whom was first a minister of the left before he became ghaus upon the death of the previous incumbent. They were followed by Hasan and Husain ('Ali's sons, the second and third imams, respectively, in Shi'ism). The line continued down to 'Abd al-Qadir Jilani. He was last "great" ghaus (*ghausiyat-e kubra*). All who followed after him were deputies (*na'ib*). In this chain of spiritual authority, the sources of spiritual knowledge are united with those of shari'a knowledge – for the source of the latter is none other than the Prophet, followed by the first four caliphs of Sunni Islam. This is a fitting image for one who, like Ahmad Riza Khan, saw himself as embodying the path of both shari'a and sufism (*tariqa*).

Shaikh 'Abd al-Qadir Jilani was also a relative of the Prophet, being descended on his mother's side from Husain ('Ali's younger son by the Prophet's daughter Fatima) and on his father's from Hasan ('Ali's older son by Fatima). This is the source of the epithet "Hasan al-Husain." This double genealogical connection mattered greatly to Shaikh 'Abd al-Qadir's followers, for they believed him to have inherited the spiritual achievements of all his ancestors.

Ahmad Riza's views on Shaikh 'Abd al-Qadir are expressed in several poems, some of which relate to his exalted status:

> Except for divinity and prophethood
> you encompass all perfections, O Ghaus.

> Who is to know what your head looks like
> as the eye level of other saints corresponds to the sole of
>   your foot?

Or:

> You are mufti or the shar', qazi of the community
> and expert in the secrets of knowledge, 'Abd al-Qadir.

Or again:

> Prophetic shower, 'Alawi season, pure garden
> Beautiful flower, your fragrance is lovely.

> Prophetic shade, 'Alawi constellation, pure station
> Beautiful moon, your radiance is lovely.

> Prophetic sun, 'Alawi mountain, pure quarry
> Beautiful ruby, your brilliance is lovely.
> (Ahmad Riza Khan, 1976: 234)

All the adjectives refer to specific persons, namely, Muhammad ("prophetic"), his cousin and son-in-law 'Ali ("'Alawi"), his daughter Fatima ("pure"), and his grandsons Hasan ("beautiful," the literal meaning of *hasan*) and Husain ("lovely," *husain* being the diminutive of *hasan*). These five figures, popularly symbolized by the human hand in Shi'ism (the *panj*), are particularly holy to Shi'i Muslims.

This emphasis on Shi'i figures of authority in the poetry of a religious leader who prided himself on his *Sunni* identity may seem odd to readers familiar with the Sunni–Shi'i divide in Muslim history. Ahmad Riza's own writings are on many occasions fiercely anti-Shi'i in tone. Nevertheless, the sufi chains of authority in all the South Asian orders – the Chishti and Naqshbandi as well, though the Qadiri more emphatically so – bring the two sides together by their emphasis on genealogy.

LOVE OF THE PROPHET

Muhammad became an object of devotion early in Islamic history, perhaps as early as the eighth century, within a hundred years of the birth of Islam. It displayed itself, among other things, in the birth of the concept of the Prophet's light (*nur-e muhammadi*), the idea that Muhammad was created out of God's light and that his creation preceded that of Adam and the world in general. In the tenth century, the famous Baghdadi mystic al-Hallaj (d. 922) wrote that the Prophet was the "cause and goal of creation." He supported his assertion by quoting the *hadith qudsi* (a hadith in which the Prophet reports a statement by God but which does not form part of the Qur'an), that "If you had not been, I would not have created the heavens." The idea of the prophetic light (on which, see Schimmel, 1975: 215–16; Schimmel, 1987) has been developed in both Sunni and Shi'i mysticism, though with an important difference. In Sunni Islam, the prophetic light belonged to the Prophet alone, whereas in Shi'ism it was inherited and carried forward by each of the twelve Imams. Among Sunni mystics, it eventually came to be connected with the concept of "annihilation in the Prophet" (*fana fi'l rasul*). "The mystic no longer goes straight on his Path toward God: first he has to experience annihilation in the spiritual guide, who functions as the representative of the Prophet, then the ... 'annihilation in the Prophet,' before he can hope to reach, if he ever does, *fana fi Allah* [annihilation in Allah]" (Schimmel, 1975: 216). Somewhat later, in the thirteenth century, the Spanish mystic Ibn al-'Arabi (d. 1240) developed the concept of Muhammad as the Perfect Man (*insan kamil*), "through whom His consciousness is manifested to Himself. ... [T]he created spirit of Muhammad is ... the medium through which ...the uncreated divine spirit [expresses itself and] through which God becomes conscious of Himself in creation" (Schimmel, 1975: 224).

Of the relationship between God and the Prophet, Ahmad Riza said:

> Only the Prophet can reach God without intermediaries. This is why, on the Day of Resurrection, all the prophets, saints (*auliya*), and 'ulama will gather in the Prophet's presence and beg him to intercede for them with God. ... The Prophet cannot have an intermediary because he is perfect (*kamil*). Perfection depends on existence (*wujud*) and the existence of the world depends on the existence of the Prophet [which in turn is dependent on the existence of God]. In short, faith in the preeminence of the Prophet leads one to believe that only God has existence, everything else is his shadow. (Ahmad Riza Khan, *Malfuzat*, vol. 2, p. 58)

To those who argued that belief in the perfection of the Prophet was contrary to belief in the Oneness of God (*tawhid*), Ahmad Riza replied that "everything comes from God," that only God is intrinsic (*zat*) while everything else is extrinsic or dependent. This said, however, God chose Muhammad as "His means of bringing the extrinsic (*ghair*) world to Him. ... Muhammad distributes what He gives. What is in the one is in the other."

And on Muhammad as God's light, he said:

> God made Muhammad from His light before He made anything else. Everything begins with the Prophet, even existence (*wujud*). He was the first prophet, as God made him before He made anything else, and he was the last as well, being the final prophet. Being the first light, the sun and all light originates from the Prophet. All the atoms, stones, trees, and birds recognized Muhammad as prophet, as did Gabriel, and the other prophets. (Bihari, 1938: 96–98)

Being made of light, the Prophet Muhammad had no shadow. Ahmad Riza wrote in a fatwa, "Undoubtedly the Prophet did not have a shadow. This is clear from hadith, from the words of the 'ulama, of the [founders of the four Sunni law schools], and the learned" (Ahmad Riza Khan, 1405/1985: 51–52). He cited numerous hadith to prove the luminous quality of the Prophet's face and body, to show that flies did not settle on his body, that after he had ridden on the back of an animal, the animal did not age any further, and so on. Such miracles associated with the Prophet also have a long history in popular literature throughout the Muslim world.

Ahmad Riza wrote a number of eloquent verses about the Prophet. One, entitled *Karoron Durud* (Millions of Blessings), is well known in Pakistan today, and is recited on the Prophet's birthday:

> I am tired, you are my sanctuary
> I am bound, you are my refuge
> My future is in your hands.
> Upon you be millions of blessings.
>
> My sins are limitless,
> but you are forgiving and merciful

Forgive me my faults and offenses,
Upon you be millions of blessings.

I will call you "Lord," for you are the beloved of the Lord
There is no "yours" and "mine" between the beloved and the
    lover.

And like poets all over the Muslim world, Ahmad Riza also celebrated the Prophet's Night Journey to Jerusalem in his poetry:

You went as a bridegroom of light
on your head a chaplet of light
wedding clothes of light on your body.
(Ahmad Riza Khan, 1976: 9, 13)

The Prophet was a personal presence in Ahmad Riza's life.
When he went on his second pilgrimage in 1905–6, he spent a
month in Medina, where the Prophet is buried. Ahmad Riza
was in Medina during the Prophet's birthday celebrations.
According to his own statement, he spent almost the entire
period at the Prophet's tomb; he even met the 'ulama of Medina
there. He considered this the holiest place on earth, even sur-
passing the Ka'ba, as he wrote in the following verse:

O Pilgrims! Come to the tomb of the king of kings
You have seen the Ka'ba, now see the Ka'ba of the Ka'ba
(Ahmad Riza Khan, 1976: 96; *Malfuzat*, vol. 2, p. 47–48)

Ahmad Riza believed that the Prophet could help whoever he
wished, in whatever way he saw fit, from his tomb. (He also had
the capacity to travel in spirit to other places.) While most Sunni
'ulama believe that the Prophet will intercede with God on
Judgment Day for ordinary Muslims, Ahmad Riza believed that
the Prophet's intercession is ongoing from the grave. (The
Prophet lives a life of sense and feeling while in his grave and
spends his time in devotional prayer.) He mediates with God
every day; his ability to do so is not limited to Judgment Day.
Ahmad Riza had undertaken this second hajj particularly in the

hope of being blessed with a vision of the Prophet. And according to Bihari, this did indeed occur after he had presented the Prophet with a poem (*ghazal*) he had composed to him. In Bihari's words, "His fortune (*qismat*) awoke [on the second night of waiting]. His watchful, vigilant eyes were blessed with the presence of the Prophet"(Bihari, 1938: 43–44). He also reported having seen the Prophet in a dream (*Malfuzat*, vol. 1, p. 82–83).

Ahmad Riza also expressed his love of the Prophet in small, everyday acts. For instance, in all correspondence, fatawa, and other writings he signed himself as 'Abd al-Mustafa, meaning "Servant of the Chosen One," the latter being an epithet of the Prophet. And on one occasion he told a follower that if his heart were to be broken into two pieces, one would be found to say, "There is no God but Allah," and the other would say, "And Muhammad is His Prophet" (*Malfuzat*, vol. 3, p. 67). Together, the two phrases constitute the profession of faith for a Muslim.

SUFI RITUALS

In addition to daily acts of devotion to the sufi pir, Shaikh 'Abd al-Qadir Jilani, and the Prophet, special rituals marked their birth or deathdays. It was a time when the community came together, affirming not only their shared beliefs but also their group identity. Some of the rituals were particular to them, not being favored by the other groups.

The ritual celebration of a pir's deathday ('*urs*) was frowned upon by 'ulama such as the Ahl-e Hadith whom Ahmad Riza called "Wahhabi." Others, such as the Deobandis, held that it was in order as long as the celebrations did not involve any forbidden activities such as singing, dancing, and the use of intoxicants. Ahmad Riza would mark the occasion by recitation of the entire Qur'an (*khatma*), poetry in praise of the Prophet (*na't*), and sermons by the 'ulama. He himself would deliver a sermon at the mosque, speaking not only about Shah Al-e Rasul but also about Shaikh 'Abd al-Qadir, the founder of the Qadiri order to which he belonged, and the Prophet. The event would be reported in Rampur's Urdu newspaper, the *Dabdaba-e Sikandari*.

It lasted anywhere between four and six days. In 1912, a year in which the *Dabdaba-e Sikandari* reported on an *'urs* celebrating Nuri Miyan on his death anniversary, it lasted five days and was attended by four to five thousand people, some from distant parts of the country (this was a much smaller turnout than the usual twenty thousand, on account of confusion as to the dates of the event). Apart from the Qur'an readings and recitation of poetry in praise of the Prophet, Nuri Miyan's *'urs* featured the viewing of prized relics (*tabarrukat*) such as a hair of the Prophet or 'Ali's robe, which had come into the family's possession. These objects were also viewed forty days after the pir's death, when his successor (*sajjada nishin*) was formally installed in a ceremony known as the *dastar-bandi* ("tying of the turban"). The symbolism of this and other rituals, it is fascinating to note, bears close similarities with ceremonies associated with royalty.

Ahmad Riza's veneration for Shaikh 'Abd al-Qadir was ritually expressed through the eating of consecrated food and the drinking of consecrated water on the eleventh of every month (*gyarahwin*) in memory of his birthdate. This was done to the accompaniment of certain prayers (*durud ghausia*) and the recitation of the Qur'an while facing Baghdad (Bihari, 1938: 202–203). As with the celebration of the *'urs* in memory of one's pir, the observance of *gyarahwin* was frowned upon by some 'ulama, including those of Deoband.

The Prophet's birth anniversary was the occasion for a big joyous celebration every year (*majlis-e milad* or *milad al-nabi*). It was one of the few annual occasions when Ahmad Riza gave a sermon at the mosque in Bareilly, addressing a large gathering that overflowed the mosque's seating capacity (Bihari, 1938: 96–98). Like the other ritual occasions mentioned above – the 'urs for pirs or sufi masters and the *gyarahwin* for Shaikh 'Abd al-Qadir Jilani – some 'ulama objected to the *milad* celebrations on the grounds that it could lead to worship of the Prophet, and hence *shirk* or association of partners with Allah. As Metcalf reports, the 'ulama of Deoband tried to "avoid fixed holidays like the maulud [*milad*] of the Prophet, the 'urs of the saints," and other feasts (Metcalf, 1982: 151). The Ahl-e Hadith were even more disapproving than the Deobandi 'ulama. Not only did they prohibit the 'urs and *gyarahwin*, but they even "prohibited all pilgrimage, even that to the grave of the Prophet at Medina. ... In their emphasis on sweeping reform, they understood sufism itself, not just its excesses, to be a danger to true religion" (Metcalf, 1982: 273–274).

However, not all were as willing to condemn such ritual celebrations. Haji Imdad Ullah, mentioned earlier, had addressed the issue in his book *Faisla-e Haft Mas'ala*. In his view, the permissibility of the event depended on the intention of the participants. If a person equated the ritual with *ibadat* or worship, on a par with obligations such as ritual prayer (*namaz*) or the fast during Ramadan, then it was reprehensible. However, if it was seen as a means of honoring and respecting the Prophet, it was acceptable (*Faisla-e Haft Mas'ala*, 50–76). Another controversial issue had to do with the ceremony known as *qiyam* or "standing up" during the *milad*. This was a point at which the Prophet's birth was recalled during the sermon. Ahmad Riza justified the act of standing up as a mark of respect for the Prophet, and also quoted a scholar from Arabia who said that the Prophet's spirit was present in the room at that time.

RELATIONS WITH OTHER MUSLIMS

Ahmad Riza's relations with the other Indian reform movements are best understood with reference to his 1906 fatwa,

Husam al-Haramain, written while in Mecca. In his *Malfuzat*, Ahmad Riza explains that when he arrived in Mecca he found that the judgment of unbelief was about to be passed on an Indian scholar for having supported the argument that the Prophet had knowledge of the unseen. He suggests that had it not been for the presence of a Deobandi scholar, Maulana Khalil Ahmad Ambethwi (a disciple of Maulana Rashid Ahmad Gangohi) in Mecca, this judgment would not have been arrived at. He therefore hastened to write a fatwa of his own to avert the expected pronouncement of *kufr* (or *takfir*). As Ahmad Riza said: "the Wahhabis had arrived before [me], among them Khalil Ahmad Ambethwi. ... They had obtained access to the ministers of the kingdom, right up to the Sharif. And they had raised the issue of the [Prophet's] knowledge of the unseen" (*Malfuzat*, vol. 2, p. 8).

Ahmad Riza was anxious to present his arguments to the highest authorities in the Sunni Muslim world while he was there, for confirmation of these arguments by the Meccan 'ulama would bolster his standing at home while undermining that of his opponents. The fatwa begins by describing the sorry state of Sunni Islam in India at the time:

> The school (*madhab*) of the Ahl-e Sunnat is a stranger in India. The darkness of dissension (*fitna*) and trial is fearful; wicked- ness is in the ascendancy; mischief has triumphed. ... It is incumbent on [you] to help the religion and humiliate the miscreants, if not by the sword, then at least by the pen.
> (*Husam*: 9–10)

Later in the fatwa he makes the same point by citing a hadith in which Abu Bakr, the first Sunni caliph, is said to have heard the Prophet say that a time will come when things are so bad that a person who was a Muslim in the morning will be a *kafir* in the evening, and vice versa. This is how bad things are in India, he tells the Meccan 'ulama.

What do you think of my judgment, he asks them in urgent tones:

> Tell me clearly whether you think these leaders ... are as I have portrayed them in my commentary, and if so, whether the judgment [of unbelief] that I have passed on them is appropriate, or whether, on the contrary, it is not permissible to call them kafirs – even though they deny the fundamentals of the faith (zaruriyat-e din), ... are Wahhabis, and ... insult Allah and the Prophet. (Husam: 10)

We must pause to consider two terms used in this passage. First, what is meant by "fundamentals of the faith," and second, what exactly did Ahmad Riza mean when he called the people he accused of unbelief "Wahhabis"?

The first term is easily explained, as it was the subject of previous fatawa by Ahmad Riza which had dealt primarily with the Nadwa. As he explained there, the fundamentals (or essentials) included beliefs based on clear verses (nusus) of the Qur'an (as against verses open to a variety of interpretations), on accepted and widely known hadith, and on the consensus (ijma) of the Muslim community. Such beliefs include: the unity of Allah, the prophethood of Muhammad, heaven and hell, the delights and punishments of the grave, the questioning of the dead, the reckoning on the day of judgment, belief in the prophets, in the corporeal existence of the angels, including the Angel Gabriel through whom Muhammad received the revelations contained in the written Qur'an, in the jinn and Satan, and the occurrence of miracles. All these beliefs were "articles of faith" or aqida, and had to be accepted. As Friedmann comments with regard to Mirza Ghulam Ahmad, "Faith is ... indivisible: even the rejection of one essential article places the person beyond the pale" (Friedmann, 1989: 160). It is ironic that when this was applied by other Indian 'ulama to Mirza Ghulam Ahmad, he was judged an unbeliever. He is the first person so judged in

Husam al-Haramain. Unlike the other people named in the fatwa, however, he was not described as a "Wahhabi."

The term "Wahhabi" has been encountered in previous chapters with reference to Indian 'ulama such as Muhammad Isma'il and Sayyid Ahmad Barelwi (leaders of the Tariqa-e Muhammadiyya in the 1820s), for instance, or the Ahl-e Hadith and Sayyid Ahmad Khan (the founder of MAO College in Aligarh). Ahmad Riza was not specifically suggesting that the 'ulama he called Wahhabi had any direct link with the nineteenth-century Wahhabi movement in Arabia, though he did think that it had influenced these Indian 'ulama. He used it as a general term of abuse for anyone he deemed to be disrespectful of the Prophet.

In the rest of the fatwa, Ahmad Riza proceeded to name four groups of Indian 'ulama and explain why he considered the leader of each group to be an unbeliever. The first, as noted above, was Mirza Ghulam Ahmad, whose followers Ahmad Riza calls the Ghulamiyya (rather than Ahmadiyya, as they called themselves), in a play on words – the literal meaning of the word *ghulam* is "slave," though here it is probably better understood as "knave," as Ahmad Riza accused him of making a number of misleading claims about himself (claims we examined in chapter 2). Reversing Ghulam Ahmad's claim that he was "like the Messiah" (Jesus Christ), Ahmad Riza denigrated him as the Antichrist (*dajjal*), inspired by Satan. However, it was Ghulam Ahmad's statement that he was a "shadowy" prophet that incensed Ahmad Riza the most. His unbelief was said to be greater than that of any of the other scholars named in the fatwa.

Ahmad Riza's second group consisted of "Wahhabis" who believed that this world was only one out of seven, and that there were prophets like Muhammad in the other six worlds as well, making seven in all. He referred to this group by the home-made term *Wahhabiyya Amthaliyya*, "likeness Wahhabis." According to him, most of them held that the likenesses of Muhammad were the last prophets in their respective worlds, as Muhammad was in this one, but there were also some who denied it: in the other six worlds the "seal of the prophets" (Arabic, *khatim al-anbiya'*) would be someone else. Ahmad Riza called these people, whom he found particularly offensive, "seal Wahhabis." Ahmad Riza appears to have been referring to debates about God's unlimited power which had been ongoing since the early nineteenth century. In *Taqwiyat al-Iman* (Strengthening the Faith), Muhammad Isma'il had written:

> In a twinkling, solely by pronouncing the word "Be!" [God] can, if he like[s], create tens of millions of apostles, saints, genii, and angels, of similar ranks with Gabriel and Muhammad, or can produce a total subversion of the whole universe, and supply its place with new creations.
> (Mir Shahamat 'Ali trans., 339)

Since that time, the Indian reformist 'ulama had been debating among themselves whether this meant that there could hypothetically be other final prophets in the six other worlds they believed to exist apart from the one we know.

All three of the 'ulama Ahmad Riza described as leaders of the "likeness" or "seal" Wahhabis were from Deoband. One 'alim was quoted as saying that the discerning among the 'ulama know that prophetic superiority is unrelated to being either first or last in time. Ahmad Riza declared that they were unbelievers because they had implicitly denied the finality of the Prophet Muhammad, which of course was a "fundamental" belief on which all Muslims agreed.

The third group (whom Ahmad Riza called the "Wahhabiyya Kadhdhabiyya," "the lie Wahhabis,") also from Deoband, were said to believe that God can lie should He wish to. The leader of these 'ulama was said to be Maulana Rashid Ahmad Gangohi, the Deobandi 'alim whose fatwa on pilgrimage we examined in chapter 3. By saying that God can lie, Ahmad Riza said that Rashid Ahmad was casting doubt on the very profession of faith, the *shahada* or *kalima*. The first part of the profession says, "There is no God but God," and belief in it is, once again, necessary if one is to be considered a Muslim. Once again, Ahmad Riza's discussion ignored the hypothetical nature of Gangohi's statement, which was also about God's absolute power.

He called the last group the "Wahhabiyya Shaytaniyya", "the Satanic Wahhabis." Allegedly led by Rashid Ahmad Gangohi, like the third group, they were said to believe that Satan's knowledge exceeded that of the Prophet and that the Prophet's knowledge of the unseen was only partial. Rashid Ahmad was said to have cited a controversial hadith to the effect that the Prophet Muhammad did not even know what lay on the other side of a wall, claiming that highly respected authorities also accepted it, which Ahmad Riza doubted. In support of his own argument Ahmad Riza cited a Qur'an verse:

> He is the knower of the Unknown,
> and He does not divulge His secret to any one
> Other than an apostle He has chosen.
> (72: 26–27, Ahmed 'Ali trans.)

The suggestion that the Prophet Muhammad's superiority to preceding prophets since the beginning of time was even hypothetically denied, or that the finality of his prophethood was being denied, or that his knowledge of the unseen was not acknowledged led Ahmad Riza to declare that the 'ulama concerned were *kafirs* and apostates (*murtadd*) from Islam.

THE ACCUSATIONS OF UNBELIEF

This accusation was not lightly made. In earlier fatawa on Muhammad Isma'il and his statements in *Taqwiyat al-Imam*, for example, Ahmad Riza had cited seventy different grounds for declaring Muhammad Isma'il to be an unbeliever, but had not in fact done so. He had believed it prudent to "restrain the tongue" (kaff-e lisan) and had given Muhammad Isma'il the benefit of the doubt, as he believed one should. In 1896, he had written a fatwa in which he characterized a number of contemporary Muslim movements – from Sayyid Ahmad Khan's modernist Aligarh movement, to the Ahl-e Hadith, Deoband, and the Nadwa, not to mention the Shi'a – as having "wrong" or "bad" beliefs (bad-mazhab) and being "lost" (gumrah). These people were misleading ordinary Muslims, he said. In 1900, he had sent this fatwa (most of which was against the Nadwa) to certain Meccan 'ulama, asking them to confirm his opinions (sixteen Meccan 'ulama had signed their assent to this fatwa). But with the exception of the Aligarh modernists (whom he described as "kafirs and murtadds," he had stopped far short of calling the other groups unbelievers, even though they had, in his view, denied the "essentials" of the faith (zaruriyat-e din).

Much had changed by 1906, apparently. In 1900 a number of his followers had declared him to be the Renewer (mujaddid) of the fourteenth Islamic century. Not surprisingly, the claim was not accepted by rival movements who elevated their own 'ulama to the title. Perhaps this helps explain why it was that when Ahmad Riza went on pilgrimage in 1905–6, he was prepared to write a fatwa against a small group of Deobandi 'ulama, as well as Mirza Ghulam Ahmad, naming them all as unbelievers.

For the Ahl-e Sunnat, this effort was crowned with success when twenty 'ulama from Mecca and thirteen from Medina certified Husam al-Haramain, giving it their support. They belonged to three different law schools, namely, the Hanafi, Shafi'i, and Maliki. One of them (whose title was Shaikh al-'Ulama) appears to have been a scholar of great standing in Mecca. Khalil Ahmad Ambethwi, the Deobandi scholar who had preceded Ahmad Riza to Mecca and had been trying to get a fatwa declaring an Indian scholar to be an unbeliever because of his belief in the Prophet's knowledge of the unseen, had to leave Mecca two weeks after his arrival because, Metcalf says, some people "objected to his visit." Back in India, the Deobandis got busy writing fatawa of their own responding to Ahmad Riza "point by point," leading to what Metcalf calls a "*fatwa* war" (Metcalf, 1982: 310).

RELATIONS WITH NON-MUSLIMS: HINDUS AND THE BRITISH

With regard to Muslims' relations with Hindus, Ahmad Riza's assessment was that the interests of Hindus and Muslims were intrinsically opposed. He argued that the Muslim leaders of the Khilafat (and Noncooperation) movements had lost their sense of balance, as they wanted to cut off relations with one set of unbelievers, the British, while seeking close relations with another, the Hindus. In religious terms, this was tantamount to "pronouncing that which was indifferent (*mubah*; neither good nor bad) to be forbidden (*haram*), and that which was forbidden to be an absolute duty (*farz qati*)." The Christians were at least people of the book, whereas the Hindus were pagans.

In a 1920 fatwa about the Noncooperation movement (one of his last), he argued that even in political terms it made no sense for the Muslims to throw in their lot with the Hindus, for whereas the British had refrained from interfering in Muslims' internal (and religious) affairs, the Hindus had done the very opposite. Here he cited the incidence of recent Hindu–Muslim riots in the United Provinces, and Hindu refusal to allow the sacrifice of cows during the 'Id festivities. Criticizing the Muslim leadership bitterly, he wrote:

> What religion is this that goes from its [previously]
> incomplete subservience to the Christians to completely

shunning them, and immerses itself wholly in following the polytheists (*mushrikin*)? They [the Muslims] are running from the rain only to enter a drainpipe. (Ahmad Riza Khan, 1920: 94)

In the same fatwa, Ahmad Riza went on to argue that social relations (*mu'amalat*) with the British were permissible according to the shari'a as long as unbelief or disobedience to the shari'a were not promoted thereby. But the leaders of the Khilafat and Noncooperation movements had prohibited such relations, while simultaneously advocating intimacy with Hindus. If all relations with the British were to be cut off, he argued, then why did the Muslim leaders continue to use the railways, the telegraph, and the postal system, all of which benefited the British Indian government's revenues?

Ahmad Riza was not alone among the 'ulama to make such arguments on the basis of his interpretation of the sources. According to I. H. Qureshi (1974: 270–271), some 'ulama of Deoband were also opposed to the Noncooperation movement, but such was the atmosphere in the country that their voices were not heeded.

5

AHL-E SUNNAT INSTITUTIONS AND SPREAD OF THE MOVEMENT BEYOND BAREILLY

The Ahl-e Sunnat (or "Barelwi") movement began to take shape in the 1880s, and came into its own in the 1890s in the context of its anti-Nadwa campaign. Thereafter it grew steadily in different parts of the country, as Ahmad Riza's followers them-selves began schools, published journals, held oral disputa-tions, and organized around specific issues in different parts of the country. Being built around scholarly interpretation of the Qur'an and prophetic sunna together with sufi practice and rit-ual, its participants also encouraged the kinds of annual calen-drical observations described in chapter 4.

In this chapter I look at the organizational features of the movement, and then turn to a divisive debate that split its mem-bers along generational and political lines during World War I.

SEMINARIES (MADRASAS)

Unlike the Deobandis and the Nadwat al-'Ulama, the Ahl-e Sunnat movement did not have a central Dar al-'Ulum at

Bareilly or in any of the other small towns in the United Provinces where they were influential, although they did have small-scale, relatively modest madrasas in Bareilly and elsewhere. An important madrasa associated with the movement later on was the Dar al-'Ulum Hizb al-Ahnaf in Lahore, founded in 1924 by Sayyid Didar 'Ali Alwari (1856–1935), who belonged to the Chishti (Nizami) order of sufis. He counted Ahmad Riza as one of his teachers, having received a certificate from him in jurisprudence (*fiqh*) and hadith, among other things. Like all the other Ahl-e Sunnat madrasas, the Hizb al-Ahnaf taught the Dars-i Nizami syllabus. Amply supported by financial contributions by Panjab-based pirs, it trained large numbers ("hundreds of thousands," according to Sayyid Didar 'Ali's grandson) of 'ulama and teachers throughout Panjab. Organized along the same lines as Deoband's Dar al-'Ulum, it also had specialized departments of preaching (*tabligh*) and debate. Preachers were needed both to counter the influence of rival Muslim movements (described in the Ahl-e Sunnat literature as "Wahhabis") and the Arya Samaj. The Arya Samaj, a Hindu reformist organization founded by Swami Dayanand in the Panjab in the 1860s, had become a matter of concern for Muslim reformers in the early twentieth century, on account of its *shuddhi* or reconversion movement, that is, the effort to convert Hindus who had converted to Islam back to Hinduism. Debaters had a similar competitive function, namely, to increase Ahl-e Sunnat influence and curtail that of its rivals.

A number of smaller Ahl-e Sunnat madrasas dotted the north Indian plains: the Madrasa Manzar al-Islam in Bareilly founded by Ahmad Riza in 1904, and managed by his brother and by Zafar ud-Din Bihari, was perpetually short of funds, particularly during the war years (1914–18). In Badayun, the Madrasa Shams al-'Ulum was founded in 1899, and fared well because of a grant from the Nizam of Hyderabad (which lasted until 1948, when Hyderabad was incorporated into independent India). It also received British support in the form of land and buildings. This madrasa had a separate publications wing, and its graduates went on to pass BA examinations in Urdu and Persian at Panjab and Allahabad universities, earning the title of Maulawi 'Alim (Urdu) and Munshi Fazil (Persian). In Muradabad, Ahmad Riza's close follower Na'im ud-Din Muradabadi founded a school, the Madrasa Na'imiyya, in the 1920s. By the 1930s it had become large enough to earn the title of Jam'iyya (center of learning). It had a Dar al-Ifta (center for the writing of fatawa) and handsome buildings. In the late 1980s, I found it in the heart of Muradabad, surrounded by narrow lanes and bustling commerce. The classrooms surrounded an open court-yard, to one side of which was Na'im ud-Din's simple tomb.

These and countless other madrasas like them (many are flourishing in the Pakistani cities of Karachi, Lahore, and else-where today) are "modern" in the sense that they no longer fol-low the one-to-one style of instruction practiced until the mid-nineteenth century, and also in that they have annual examinations, classrooms, libraries, and all the other organiza-tional features of regular public schools. But the syllabus is still based on the Dars-i Nizami curriculum.

PRINTING PRESSES AND PUBLICATIONS

In the early nineteenth century, most printing presses in India were owned by Christian missionaries who used them to pub-lish copies of the Bible in Indian languages and a few classical Indian texts. By the 1880s, however, the situation had changed dramatically, as Indian-owned printing presses grew in number and Indian-language publishing blossomed. In Bareilly, two printing presses published most of Ahmad Riza Khan's fatawa and other writings between them. They were the Hasani Press, owned by Ahmad Riza's brother Hasan Riza Khan (and later by his nephew Hasnain Riza Khan), and the Matba' Ahl-e Sunnat wa Jama'at, run by Ahmad Riza's close follower Amjad 'Ali A'zami. The earlier books published date from the late 1870s. Some were only fifteen pages long, others had hundreds of pages, and most fell somewhere in between. They had print runs of between five hundred and a thousand copies, and popular titles were sometimes reprinted as many as three times. For instance, an anti-Deobandi fatwa on the need to respect graves (entitled *Ihlak al-Wahhabiyyin 'ala Tauhin Qubur al-Muslimin,* or Ruin to the Wahhabis for their Disrespect toward Muslim Graves) was first published in 1904, and reprinted for the fourth time in 1928 with a print run of a thousand. Given the fact that books were often read aloud (since there were many more people who could not read than those who could), the reach of a single copy was much greater than is apparent from the numbers.

Much care was expended in finding an appropriate title, the beginning and end of which not only rhymed but also poked fun at the opponent. For example, in 1896 Hasan Riza Khan, the owner of the Hasani Press, wrote an anti-Nadwa work entitled *Nadwe ka Tija – Rudad-e Som ka Natija* (The Nadwa's *Tija* – The Result of Its Third Report). The word *tija* means the third day after a person's death. Thus, Hasan Riza implied that the Nadwa's third report showed that the Nadwa was dead as an institution. (Ahmad Riza alone wrote more than two hundred fatawa against the Nadwa.) Furthermore, the numerical value of the individual letters (in accordance with the *abjad* system, which assigns each letter of the Arabic alphabet a number) yielded the date of the work when added together.

Journals were another category of publication. In Patna, Qazi 'Abd ul-Wahid Azimabadi, a close follower, started publishing a monthly journal, the *Tuhfa-e Hanafiyya* (Hanafi Gift) in 1897–8, with the primary purpose of rebutting the Nadwa. It carried articles about tenets of the faith, jurisprudence, hadith, stories about the prophets and the first caliphs, and reports about rival 'ulama organizations, particularly the Nadwa. It had a small circulation (of two hundred to two hundred and fifty), its subscribers being the educated elite (*ru'asa*, sing. *ra'is*) of towns in Bihar, the United Provinces, Bombay, Ahmadabad, and Hyderabad.

Newspapers constituted yet another kind of Ahl-e Sunnat publication. Here I am thinking particularly of the Rampur-based *Dabdaba-e Sikandari* (in translation, Alexander's [Awesome] Majesty), which began weekly publication in the 1860s. I examined issues dating from 1908 to 1917. The paper had a pro-British perspective, which paralleled that of the Nawab of Rampur (though it was privately owned by a scholar of the Chishti (Sabiri) line of sufis; the nawab probably patronized the paper, but he did not own it). In its international political coverage, the *Dabdaba* reported on the war and other major events in Europe, as well as national events in India (such as the constitutional devolution of power to Indians in the early twentieth century), particularly those of interest to Muslims. In addition, it devoted space to purely "religious" events, such as *'urs* announcements, detailed reports on a divisive debate within the Ahl-e Sunnat movement about the call to prayer (see pp. 118–22), and, during Ramadan, the exact time of sunrise and sunset as determined by the 'ulama. Starting in 1910, it also devoted two full pages (out of sixteen) to fatawa by the Ahl-e Sunnat 'ulama in answer to questions. By February 1912, it had published two hundred such fatawa.

VOLUNTARY ASSOCIATIONS AND ORAL DEBATES

Finally, let us look at two other kinds of activities less dependent on the written word, namely, voluntary associations and oral debates, common to all the reform movements of the late nineteenth century. The organizational structure of voluntary associations, like that of the madrasas, showed clear British influence, in that each had office bearers, annual reports, fundraising committees, and so on. To quote Kenneth Jones on the Arya Samaj, "Battles were fought, victories won, and defeats suffered according to the proper forms of parliamentary procedure" between the rival "sabhas, samajes, clubs, anjumans, and societies" which proliferated in this period (Jones, 1976: 318–319).

Thus in 1921, the Ahl-e Sunnat 'ulama formed an organization called "Ansar al-Islam" (Helpers of Islam, the word "Ansar" being a reference to the seventh-century helpers of the Prophet at Medina) in order to raise money for the Ottomans after their defeat at the hands of the Allies in World War I. It was but one of several such Indian organizations, and was in competition with the Farangi Mahall-led (and much better known) Anjuman-e Khuddam-e Ka'ba (Society of the Servants of the Ka'ba). Another organization, the Jama'at-e Riza-e Mustafa (Society Pleasing to the Prophet Muhammad), was formed around 1924 in order to counter the conversion efforts of the Arya Samaj.

Oral disputations (munazara) were perhaps the oldest form of contestation between rival groups, both Hindu and Muslim. In the early nineteenth century, the contestation had been between Christian missionaries on the one hand and Hindu or Muslim learned men on the other. In the latter half of the century, by contrast, the contestants were often adherents of the same religion, challenging each other's version of reform. The disputations were highly public events observed by large numbers of onlookers, and thus they had the air of a fair (mela). They lasted several hours, sometimes several days. Although neither side was ever won over, both usually left feeling they had won. Here is the description of a disputation between an Ahl-e Sunnat contestant and a Deobandi one, from the Ahl-e Sunnat perspective:

In 1919–1920, [Ahmad Riza] sent Hashmat 'Ali to debate
with [a Deobandi 'alim] at Haldwani Mandi, all by himself.
He was only nineteen years old. He harassed his opponent
and silenced his argument [in defense of a Deobandi book].
And on the question of the Prophet's knowledge of the unseen,
[the opponent] was left astounded. This was his first debate. . . .
After successfully defeating his opponent, he returned to
[Ahmad Riza, who] was very pleased with his report, embraced
him, and prayed for him. He gave him the name "the father of
success," as well as a turban and tunic, and five rupees. He also
said that henceforth [Hashmat 'Ali] would get five rupees every
month. . . . And, by the grace of Allah, [Ahmad Riza's] favor was
always with him, and he won a debate on every occasion.
(Mahbub 'Ali Khan, 1960: 7–8)

The following reports on a disputation between the Ahl-e
Sunnat and Swami Shraddhanand, leader of the Arya Samaj,
that never took place:

When Shraddhanand began [the conversion movement],
Hazrat [Na'im ud-Din Muradabadi] invited him to a debate.
He accepted the invitation. Hazrat went to Delhi [to debate
with him]. He ran from there and came to Bareilly. Hazrat
went to Bareilly and challenged him to debate. He ran from
there and went to Lucknow. When Hazrat went to Lucknow,
he went to Patna. Hazrat followed him to Patna, but he went
to Calcutta. Hazrat went there too, and caught [up with] him.
He then clearly refused to debate. (Na'imi, 1959: 9)

The point was made: Swami Shraddhanand knew he would lose
if he debated with Na'im ud-Din Muradabadi but could not
refuse the challenge thrown at him. The disputations had an
element of "social inversion," a term used by scholars who have
studied public theater to describe occasions when the normal
social etiquette observed between equals is dispensed with,
giving each party license to insult the other. Occasionally, the
disputations led to violence.

GENERATIONAL FISSURES IN
THE MOVEMENT

In January 1914, alongside news of impending war in Europe and national events in British India, the Rampur newspaper *Dabdaba-e Sikandari* began to report a very local story. The issue, which had evidently been agitating the 'ulama of Bareilly and a number of local country towns – all of whom identified with the Ahl-e Sunnat movement – for some time before it began to be reported in the paper, had to do with the Friday noontime prayer, the most important of all the weekly prayers.

The Friday noontime prayer is distinguished by the fact that the call to it is sounded twice rather than once. The question was: should the muezzin, the one who issues the call, be standing inside the mosque or outside it when he makes the second call? According to Ahmad Riza, he should be standing outside the mosque, for this had been the practice since the time of the Prophet and the first two caliphs. He cited a hadith from Abu Daud in support of his view. Opposing him were 'ulama from towns near Bareilly, such as Rampur, Pilibhit, and Badayun. They argued that the second *azan* had been sounded from within the mosque since the beginnings of Islam and that there was no reason to change the practice now.

The space devoted to this dispute in the *Dabdaba-e Sikandari* indicates that it had been brewing for some time. In January 1914, Ahmad Riza addressed a number of related questions: what had been the precedent and model (*sunnat*) set by the Prophet and his closest companions? What should be done when the prevailing practice contravened this ideal? Should people change their practice to conform to the ideal?

Ahmad Riza's response – that the current practice of sounding the call from within the mosque was mere custom (*rawaj*) and had no basis in either the Qur'an or the hadith, and that it was the 'ulama's moral duty to "revive a dead sunnat" – was followed by a request that supporters of his view let the Dar al-Ifta at Bareilly know. They were also asked to collect the signatures of those who had decided to follow his lead, and to send them on to the Dar al-Ifta.

Two weeks after Ahmad Riza's January fatwa, his opponents countered that the practice of sounding a second azan had not existed during the Prophet's time. They said it had been started by the third caliph, Caliph 'Uthman (r. 644–56), and that it had been done from within the mosque for thirteen hundred years: far from reviving a dead sunnat, Ahmad Riza and his followers were "kill[ing] a living sunnat. And far from getting a reward, [they] would be punished." Ahmad Riza Khan was basing his view on his own independent reasoning (ijtihad), they claimed; it was the consensus of the community that ought to prevail, not the opinion of a single scholar. Given that Ahmad Riza – like the majority of Indian 'ulama – laid no claim to exercising ijtihad, and that he believed firmly in staying within the confines of the Hanafi law school, eschewing even the mixing of law schools after the fashion of Ashraf 'Ali Thanawi (see p. 70), this was a particularly offensive charge.

In subsequent months the debate grew more heated as accusations proliferated on both sides. Ahmad Riza argued that the 'ulama opposing him were misleading the people, "turning their backs on religion [din]," "slandering the shari'a," "following a bid'a" rather than a sunna, and "committing a grave sin." In a later issue of the Dabdaba, he accused a particular scholar of being influenced by certain Deobandi 'ulama. A follower of Ahmad Riza's offered a Deobandi scholar a fifty-rupee prize if he was able to satisfactorily answer a list of questions related to the second azan. The debate was thus widening beyond the original group of contestants.

In February 1915, Ahmad Riza successfully secured the signatures of a small number of 'ulama from the Haramain assenting to his point of view. One of the Medinan scholars wrote: "There is no advantage to giving the *azan* in the mosque. Those people who are outside [are alerted by the *azan* that they] should strive after the remembrance of Allah." It was also reported that pamphlets were now being written by both sides. The opponents now included 'ulama who considered themselves Ahl-e Sunnat as well as Deobandis, as some Ahl-e Sunnat 'ulama began to defect to the other side. The use of pamphlets was also significant, as a pamphlet might reach more people than either a fatwa or a newspaper. Being intended for a wider audience than a small erudite circle of 'ulama, it might also be written in a looser, more informal style. (On the other hand, it must be admitted that fatawa were often published in the form of little booklets or pamphlets for general circulation as well.)

The next stage in the debate was quite dramatic: sometime in 1916 a court case was instituted against Ahmad Riza in Badayun on a charge of libel. The details are unclear, but the plaintiff charged that one of Ahmad Riza's pamphlets (entitled *Sad al-Firar*, A Hundred Flights [i.e., Defeats]) was libelous of Maulana 'Abd ul-Muqtadir Badayuni, who had recently died. This was a surprising development, because the latter came from a family with close ties with Ahmad Riza's own. Moreover, Maulana 'Abd ul-Muqtadir had played a prominent part at the 1900 meeting in Patna at which Ahmad Riza had been proclaimed *mujaddid*, having initiated that proclamation.

In 1917 Ahmad Riza was summoned to court, but failed to appear. This was a clear indication that he did not acknowledge the authority of the court. His reasons included the public setting of a British Indian court, in which British Indian law rather than shari'a law was applied, and one in which the judge himself was usually a non-Muslim (in this case it was a Hindu). Some months later the judge dismissed the case, saying the plaintiff had no grounds for his case. Ahmad Riza's supporters interpreted this judgment as a victory, and the event was celebrated with the group recitation of verses in praise of the

Prophet (na't) and victory processions in Bareilly. There ended the "azan debate," as no appeal was filed. (Nevertheless, the actual practice of calling the second azan from within rather than outside the mosque did not change either.)

This debate shows us how the community, in the sense of the people who actually interacted and took account of each other, had become vastly bigger than it used to be and now included people who were linked by newspapers and other modern communications. It probably started as an oral discussion in Bareilly, then moved on to debate in the Rampur newspaper, then widened further still when Ahmad Riza received approval for his point of view from Mecca and Medina, and finally moved to a British Indian court where he was charged with libel. The audience increased substantially after the Rampur paper began reporting on it in 1914. The paper was probably read by the literate Muslim classes throughout the modern state of Uttar Pradesh – by 'ulama, landed gentry, and urban professionals. These people, who had probably heard of Ahmad Riza even if they did not know of him personally, became part of a "consuming public" – following Benedict Anderson's insights in *Imagined Communities* – through their act of reading the paper.

It was characteristic of this public that it was anonymous, unlike the initial group of people close to Ahmad Riza, whose loyalty he could count on. Public opinion had to be won over. Presentation of validating opinions from Mecca and Medina was important in the Indian context precisely because it could be expected to carry weight outside the circle of people bound to Ahmad Riza by personal ties. In the final stage of debate, that centered on the courtroom, the issue became even more public and, for the first time, political as well, in the sense that the authority of the colonial state was being pitted against that of a traditional scholar.

The fissures in the Ahl-e Sunnat movement, evident at the conclusion of the azan debate, were occurring at a time of

enormous political change in British India. The politicization of
the Muslim community had begun even before World War I –
witness not only the organizational efforts of 'Abd ul-Bari
(see p. 78), but also the Kanpur mosque dispute and riot in
1913, in which the Sunni Muslims of Kanpur, a major city in the
United Provinces, angrily protested against the demolition by
the British Indian government of part of a mosque in order to
make way for a road. The issues that arose after the war –
whether or not to join the Indian National Congress, or form a
joint party of 'ulama from different movements, or abstain
from politics altogether – were to grow in urgency after
Ahmad Riza's death in 1921. The new leaders of the movement
adopted different solutions and led their followers in different
directions. While no single person was able to unite the Ahl-e
Sunnat movement as Ahmad Riza had done, this was perhaps a
sign of the success of the movement rather than the reverse,
illustrating its geographic spread and growth far beyond
Bareilly, its original birthplace.

ASSESSMENT OF THE IMPORTANCE
OF THE MOVEMENT IN RELATION TO
OTHER MOVEMENTS

There are no statistics to tell us which of the rival reform movements of the late nineteenth and early twentieth centuries had
the most followers, particularly in the early twentieth century.
Most scholars believe that the Deobandis were influential in the
urban areas, while the "Barelwis," as the Ahl-e Sunnat are
widely known, were popular in the countryside. If this were
true, it would make the Ahl-e Sunnat vastly more influential
than the Deobandis, and probably the erudite Ahl-e Hadith as
well, not to mention the followers of Sayyid Ahmad Khan,
as the South Asian population was and continues to be

overwhelmingly rural. However, this judgment arises from the general identification of the "Barelwis" with sufism, and with unreformed Islamic practice among the population at large. But since we have no way of knowing whether Muslims who prayed at the sufi shrines that are ubiquitous throughout South Asia thought of themselves as "Barelwi," we cannot make this assumption.

How we name things affects how we think about them. Those who think of "Barelwis" think of a general sufi-oriented group of people with a vast popular following. However, if we keep the self-image of "Ahl-e Sunnat" before us, we see the movement as more focused and less diffuse. In my view, we have to start by looking at those who identified with the movement by attending its schools, subscribing to and buying its journals, attending its meetings, and participating in other ways in the issues that engaged its leadership. In addition, considering that the people who did these things were part of the literate elite, by definition a small minority, we can assume that a larger number of people around them were influenced by being read aloud to, and by constituting a silent audience that attended and participated in events. Even when we add these people in, the membership of the Ahl-e Sunnat movement could not have exceeded thousands, perhaps tens of thousands, particularly in the late nineteenth century.

Some examples will help put this in perspective. Thus, as noted earlier in the discussion of Ahl-e Sunnat publications, in the 1890s a strong anti-Nadwa campaign was waged by a follower of Ahmad Riza's in Patna, Bihar, through the journal *Tuhfa-e Hanafiyya* (Hanafi Gift). Its circulation at its height was about two hundred and fifty. Most of its subscribers in its early days were from Bihar (72 out of 119), followed by the United Provinces (23). Their professions included legal representatives, revenue collectors, students, mosque leaders, and school administrators, among others. Another example is provided by the printing history of an anti-Deobandi fatwa by Ahmad Riza dealing with the Deobandis' alleged disrespect for graves and gravesites (*Ihlak al-Wahhabiyyin 'ala Tauhin Qubur al-Muslimin*, Ruin to the Wahhabis for Their Disrespect toward Muslim Graves). It went through four printings between 1904 and 1928; a thousand copies were printed in the fourth printing (we have no numbers for the earlier editions).

Given that Ahmad Riza Khan was less interested in schools than were the Deobandis, the school network of the latter was wider and more influential than that of the Ahl-e Sunnat. To cite some rough numbers: the Madrasa Manzar al-Islam in Bareilly graduated between four and ten students per year between 1908 and 1917. Resources were poor, with few teachers, classrooms, and inadequate library and boarding facilities. Schools run by Ahmad Riza's followers in other north Indian towns also tended to be relatively modest, though as indicated above they increased steadily through the years. By comparison, by 1900 the Dar al-'Ulum at Deoband had about a dozen teachers and between two and three hundred students in a given year, new buildings, including classrooms and boarding facilities, and it graduated about fifteen thousand students in its first hundred years (1867–1967). It also had a wide network of affiliated schools, starting in 1866 with a school at Saharanpur, just north of Deoband in the western part of the Northwestern Provinces. Although its student numbers were small (about a hundred), the network was constantly growing.

Numbers for other aspects of the two movements are hard to specify, though they can be assumed to have been similar. In general, the two were often paired as oppositional groups: thus, "Deobandi–Barelwi" was a common term for sectarianism within the Indian Muslim fold.

The Ahl-e Sunnat side gained additional strength from another quarter, namely, reformist sufi groups which supported them on specific issues. Reformist sufis (of the

Naqshbandi and Chishti orders) were distinguished from the vast populace by their insistence on adherence to the shari'a and a general concern for reform. In the Panjab, a state with wealthy sufi hospices, such sufis had great influence. To cite an example, Pir Mehr 'Ali Shah of Golra (1856–1937), a small town in the Panjab, who was directly associated with the Ahl-e Sunnat movement, went to the Northwestern Provinces to study Qur'anic exegesis (*tafsir*) and hadith under reformist 'ulama, then returned to Golra to transform it into a reformist Chishti center. Anti-British in his politics, he instructed his followers to be personally observant and promoted knowledge of religious law among his followers. He often issued fatawa on points of religious law. His self-identification with the Ahl-e Sunnat added to the influence of the movement in Panjab state.

To sum up, the reformist groups had different regional emphases but more or less equal overall importance in the country as a whole, particularly in the Northwestern Provinces (renamed the United Provinces of Agra and Oudh in 1900). However, because the Deobandis emphasized schools more than the Ahl-e Sunnat, in the long term they had greater influence in the urban areas than the Ahl-e Sunnat.

6

AHMAD RIZA'S LEGACY

Ahmad Riza Khan, leader of the Ahl-e Sunnat or "Barelwi" movement, was quintessentially South Asian. The movement he led made universalist claims, as its very name makes clear. Translated, the term Ahl-e Sunnat wa Jama'at means "the devotees of the Prophet's practice and the broad community." It resonates with Sunni Muslims the world over, and has been used in the past by Sunni Muslim movements in different historical contexts and geographical settings as a means of identifying their own community with that of the first Muslims established by the Prophet in seventh-century Arabia. It was Ahmad Riza's firm belief that he was following in the path of the Prophet, and in everything he did and said he considered the Prophet his model. To those who agreed, this made him, Ahmad Riza, a model for emulation in his turn.

Ahmad Riza's interpretation of the sunna of the Prophet was informed by ideas of hierarchy and religiosity derived from sufi notions of "love" for the Prophet, and expressed itself in ritual worship centered on sufi shrines and calendrical anniversaries of sufi pirs, Shaikh 'Abd ul-Qadir Jilani, and, of course, the Prophet's birthday. It was thus informed by personal devotion to a wide array of pious and holy ancestors. This was its hallmark and its source of strength. A warm, loving (and simultaneously demanding) relationship between each believer and his or her pir lay at its heart. Such a relationship is particularly resonant in the South Asian context, for it mirrors similar ties among other religious communities in the subcontinent, particularly Hindu followers of the *bhakti* tradition. *Bhakti* or devotional worship of God emphasized the individual believer's relationship with a personal god (forms of Vishnu or Shiva). "The devotee's ... adoration was often focused on the person of a human guru or spiritual preceptor who was revered as a living manifestation of the god" (Bayly, 1989: 41). In fact, south Indian sufi texts since the fifteenth century have frequently interwoven Hindu and Muslim sufi motifs, enabling the Muslim saint to "leap the boundaries between 'Hindu' and 'non-Hindu', 'Islamic' and 'un-Islamic'"(Bayly, 1989: 120). Critics of the Ahl-e Sunnat also claim that ritual practices during the Prophet's birth celebrations *(milad)* resemble Hindu worship practices. Indeed, despite some major differences between the two traditions, such as the lack of images and of priests in the Islamic context, there are many similarities: for instance, food and water offered to and consecrated by the saint, then consumed by the worshiper, the sprinkling of rose petals in the sanctum, the recitation of religious texts and the telling of exemplary stories about the Prophet and the saints are similar to Hindu worship practices.

Nevertheless, I take seriously the Ahl-e Sunnat claim to be a reformist movement. While critics might argue that the Ahl-e Sunnat were too accommodating of local practice, too local, and too parochial to be considered "reformist" – unlike the Deobandis or the Ahl-e Hadith or the Nadwa, for example – I would argue that the Ahl-e Sunnat movement was reformist in the self-consciousness of its practice, and in its insistence on following the sunna of the Prophet at all times. In paying attention to every detail of their comportment on a daily basis, members of the Ahl-e Sunnat were no different from followers of rival movements at the time. What set them apart from the other movements was their interpretation of what, in practice, was entailed by following the Prophet's example. While they interpreted this in more custom-laden terms than their rivals, in their view they never transgressed the boundaries of the shari'a at any time.

While the Ahl-e Sunnat movement was certainly more inclined toward the emotional or magical than the Deobandi, both shared a common worldview. Ahmad Riza was punctilious about observing the sunna, as he interpreted it, in every detail of his life, and taught his followers to do likewise. Frowning on what he considered *be-shar'* (without shari'a) behavior, he dressed, walked, and conducted himself with others in ways that conformed with what he took to be the shari'a. Public events such as the *milad* and *'urs* were also conducted within the bounds of shari'a – without use of drugs and intoxicants and *qawwali* singing (though the latter was allowed in small groups by some 'ulama), and emphasizing Qur'an readings and the recitation of poetry in honor of the Prophet. Like the other reform movements, he and the Ahl-e Sunnat 'ulama in general also encouraged their followers to fulfill the five "pillars" of Islam and to refrain from antisocial behavior of any kind.

AHMAD RIZA'S *'URS* IN INDIA AND PAKISTAN

Since his death in 1921, Ahmad Riza's *'urs* has been celebrated by his followers every year in Bareilly. In 1987, I was in Bareilly during the *'urs*. Here is a transcription from my notes:

> I attended one session of the three-day annual 'urs
> celebrations for Ahmad Riza and his son Mustafa Riza.
> Women are discouraged, though not prohibited, from going. I
> was amazed at the size of the crowd. A newspaper report the
> next day said that lakhs, or hundreds of thousands, of people
> had attended. The program consisted of three days of

speeches, interspersed with Qur'an readings and recitation of na't poetry in praise of the Prophet.

The venue is a large open ground adjacent to the local college, which suspends classes for the duration of the 'urs and makes the classrooms available to people to sleep in at night. So for three days the place is like a large camp, with provision for food and shelter for some thousands of people. I didn't get to see what went on in the khanqah itself, because of the crowd. It is down in the heart of the city, accessed through narrow lanes and alleys, and there was no way one could force one's way through – my host and guide was most reluctant to attempt it.

In Pakistan, I found that Ahmad Riza's death anniversary was also commemorated with conferences at five-star hotels at which speeches were made and na't poetry recited. There are a number of Pakistani organizations which sponsor events honoring Ahmad Riza's life and work throughout the year as well as publishing his books. One of the most prominent of these, called Idara-e Minhaj al-Quran, was headed by a law professor, Tahir ul-Qadiri, in the late 1980s. Tahir ul-Qadiri was a well-known public figure in Pakistan, as he made frequent appearances on national television, delivered speeches at mosques, and was active at conferences. At a more grassroots level, the Ahl-e Sunnat were busy building schools (madrasas) throughout the country. Zaman (2002: 235 n. 51) estimates that the number of Ahl-e Sunnat schools went up from 93 in 1971 to 1,216 in 1994. The Ahl-e Sunnat are also represented at the political level. Their party is known as the Jamiyyat al-'Ulama-e Pakistan (JUP) and its leader through the 1970s and 1980s was a well-known 'alim and pir, Maulana Shah Ahmad Nurani.

I should add, however, that the Ahl-e Sunnat in Pakistan appear to be less prominent nationally than the Deobandis. Their perspective on sufism being at odds with that of the Saudi regime, they have not benefited from Saudi munificence as have other reformist groups (Zaman, 2002).

AHL-E SUNNAT/BARELWIS IN THE DIASPORA

It is not only in Pakistan that the Ahl-e Sunnat are active. They are well represented in other parts of the world as well, chiefly Great Britain, where immigration from the subcontinent has been sizeable since independence. The late 1960s saw a transformation in the South Asian Muslim immigrant population as a whole, as immigrants began to see themselves for the first time as permanent settlers rather than temporary migrants. As male workers were joined by their families, the need was felt for institutional structures – chiefly mosques and schools – which would allow community life to flourish. My comments are limited to the Muslims of Bradford, a northern industrial city representative in many ways of the overall picture.

In 1973, Pir Maroof, a prominent Ahl-e Sunnat leader, founded the World Islamic Mission (WIM), "an umbrella organization for Barelwi dignitaries, with its head office located in his mosque at Southfield Square in Bradford. ... Its first president [was] Maulana Noorani" (Lewis, 1994: 83). As Lewis explains, "the World Islamic Mission [was] clearly intended as a counterweight to the Mecca-based Muslim World League, a vehicle for those whom Barelwis scornfully dismiss as Wahhabis, whether Deobandi, Jama'at-e Islami or Ahl-i Hadith" (Lewis, 1994: 84). (The Jama'at-e Islami, founded by Maulana Mawdudi [d. 1979] in 1941, frowns upon sufi practices of the kind favored by the Ahl-e Sunnat.)

In 1989 the Muslims of Bradford were in the national – indeed, international – spotlight following the publication of

Salman Rushdie's book, *The Satanic Verses*. After an initial book-burning protest which created the impression among Britons that they were religious "fundamentalists" without furthering the British understanding of why they found the book offensive, the Bradford Council for Mosques, an umbrella group that included both Ahl-e Sunnat/Barelwis and Deobandis, tried to make its case in other ways. In 1990 the Council opened a "nationwide debate on the future of Muslims in [Britain]," and invited the Bishop of Bradford, as well as Sikh and Hindu leaders in the city, to a dialogue, hoping to enlist their support in their campaign against the book. As Lewis writes,

> The emphasis of the conference was on the need for a constructive engagement with the nation's institutions, political, social, and educational. Muslim concerns were articulated in an idiom accessible to the non-Muslim majority. ...There was a readiness to be self-critical. ... Such a conference was a tribute to the realism of the Bradford Council for Mosques and a refusal to allow Muslims to withdraw into sullen resentment. (Lewis, 1994: 164)

But this was not of course a response unique to the Ahl-e Sunnat, who formed one group of many in these events.

For all that, it is clear that the Ahl-e Sunnat movement is thriving wherever there are South Asian Muslims. Today it has its own websites, as do its competitors, so that one can follow the issues engaging its adherents at any time simply by searching the World Wide Web. At the present time, its greatest challenge appears to be to find common ground with other reformist Muslim movements and to promote understanding of its perspective among non-Muslims, whose lack of knowledge of the Muslim world leads them to see all Muslims as the same, and in a negative light. In this day and age, the need for better understanding couldn't be greater.

GLOSSARY

'alim (pl. 'ulama) scholar of Islamic law

'amm (pl. 'awamm) ordinary (in the plural, refers to ordinary people)

azan call to prayer

bid'a reprehensible innovation, opposite of *sunna*

dar ul-harb enemy territory; opposite of *dar ul-Islam*

dar ul-Islam land where Islamic law (*shari'a*) is in force

dastar-bandi "tying of the turban," ceremony marking the end of a person's studies or apprenticeship to a sufi master

din the faith; opposite of *dunya*, the world

faqih jurisprudent, one who is knowledgeable in the law

fatwa (pl. fatawa) legal opinion given by a *mufti*

hadith traditions or stories traced to the Prophet

hajj pilgrimage to Mecca, one of the five "pillars" of Islam

ijma consensus of scholars which constitutes one of the sources of Islamic law

ijtihad independent inquiry to establish the legality of a particular matter in *shari'a* terms

jihad struggle, can be internal (spiritual) or external (against an aggressor)

khalifa Caliph (during Ottoman rule); also a successor to a sufi master

khass (pl. khawass) special, the opposite of *'amm*

khutba sermon delivered by an *'alim* at Friday noontime prayer

madhhab legal tradition or school, of which there are four among Sunni Muslims

madrasa a religious academy, where the Islamic sciences are taught

manqulat the "copied" sciences, especially *hadith*

mansab/mansabdari a Mughal rank, or the holder of that rank

ma'qulat the philosophical or rational sciences

milad celebration of the Prophet's birth anniversary

mujaddid Renewer of the *shari'a*, expected at the start of every new Islamic century

na't poetry in praise of the Prophet

nawab a Mughal noble, or semi-independent Muslim ruler during Mughal times

pir sufi master, one who has *murids* or disciples

qadi judge who applies Islamic law in a court

Sayyid descendant of the Prophet

shaikh "elder" or "leader," in South Asia a title often used of a sufi master

shari'a sacred law of Islam

Shi'a/Shi'i followers of the Prophet's son-in-law 'Ali, and other Shi'i *imams*

shirk idolatry, associating partners with God

sufi Muslim mystic

sunna the "way" or "path" of the Prophet Muhammad, as known to Muslims through the *hadith* literature

taqlid following one of the Sunni law schools in preference to *ijtihad*

tariqa sufi order

tawhid unity or oneness of God

'urs celebration of a saint's death anniversary

wahdat al-shuhud "unity of appearance," a sufi concept

wahdat al-wujud "unity of being," a contrasting idea

zakat mandatory alms-tax on accrued wealth

MAJOR LANDMARKS IN SOUTH ASIAN HISTORY
From the Eighteenth to the Twentieth Century (to 1947)*

EIGHTEENTH CENTURY

1707 Aurangzeb dies in the Deccan.

1709 Nadir Shah and Ahmad Khan Abdali conquer Herat, Kabul, Panjab.

1733 Bengal independent from Mughals.

1747 Durranis (Afghan dynasty created by Ahmad Khan Abdali) conquer Delhi. Mughals under Awadh's protection.

1757 East India Company becomes *zamindar* of 24 Parganas, Bengal, after victory at the Battle of Plassey.

1765 British *nawabi* of Bengal and Bihar.

1772 Rohillas independent until 1792, then come under Awadh's protection.

1773 Awadh becomes a native state under the British.

1793 Permanent Settlement in Bengal.

---

* Adapted from David Ludden, *India and South Asia: A Short History* (Oxford: Oneworld, 2002), pp. 111–112, 148–149, 198, and 212.

1798 Hyderabad becomes a native state under the British.

1799 British defeat Tipu Sultan of Mysore.

NINETEENTH CENTURY

1801 Madras Presidency formed. Rampur becomes a native state in former Rohilkhand.

1803 British conquer Delhi and make it a dependency.

1804 Rohillas absorbed by Awadh.

1818 Marathas conquered by British, and their territory forms the bulk of Bombay Presidency.

1835 Macaulay's Minute on Education. English becomes the official language of government and the courts.

1857 The Revolt or "Mutiny" sweeps across north India. Calcutta, Bombay, and Madras Universities founded.

1858 India comes under Crown rule.

1867 Dar al-'Ulum founded at Deoband.

1875 Arya Samaj founded by Swami Dayanand. Muhammadan Anglo-Oriental (MAO) College founded in Aligarh by Sayyid Ahmad Khan.

1885 Indian National Congress founded.

TWENTIETH CENTURY (TO 1947)

1905 Partition of Bengal. Anti-Partition protests.

1906 All-India Muslim League founded at Dhaka.

1911 Delhi Durbar; Bengal Partition revoked; capital moved from Calcutta to Delhi.

1914 Gandhi returns to India from South Africa;
World War I starts; Indian troops sent overseas.

1919 Khilafat movement launched.

1920 Non-Cooperation movement; Hijrat movement to
Afghanistan.

1921 Dyarchy established.

1930 Round Table conferences 1930 and 1932;
Salt Satyagraha.

1932 Second civil disobedience movement. Communal
Award. Gandhi's Poona Pact with B. R. Ambedkar.

1935 Government of India Act.

1937 Elections in India. Congress ministries formed in
seven provinces. Muslim League reorganized.

1939 World War II starts. Congress ministries resign.
Muslim League declares "Deliverance Day."

1940 Muslim League adopts Lahore Resolution stating goal
of creating Pakistan.

1941 Jama'at-e Islami founded by Maulana Maududi.

1942 Quit India movement.

1943 Bengal famine (to 1944).

1946 Cabinet Mission; violence in Bengal; elections.
Muslim League wins Muslim-majority areas;
Lord Mountbatten comes to India as Viceroy.

1947 Independence for India and Pakistan; violence in
Panjab and Bengal; mass migration and massacre of
populations; Kashmir accedes to India.

BIBLIOGRAPHY

Ahmad Khan, Muin ud-Din. *History of the Fara'izi Movement in Bengal (1818–1906)*. Karachi: Pakistan Historical Society, 1965.

Anderson, Benedict. *Imagined Communities: Reflections on the Origin and Spread of Nationalism*. London: Verso, 1983.

Bayly, Susan. *Saints, Goddesses and Kings: Muslims and Christians in South Indian Society, 1700–1900*. Cambridge: Cambridge University Press, 1989.

Bihari, Zafar ud-Din. *Hayat-e A'la Hazrat*. Vol. 1. Karachi: Maktaba Rizwiyya, 1938.

Cohn, Bernard S. *Colonialism and Its Forms of Knowledge: The British in India*. Princeton: Princeton University Press, 1996.

Cole, J. R. I. *Roots of North Indian Shi'ism in Iran and Iraq: Religion and State in Awadh, 1722–1839*. Delhi: Oxford University Press, 1989.

Denny, Frederick M. *An Introduction to Islam*. New York: Macmillan, 1985.

Ewing, Katherine. 1980. "The *Pir* or Sufi Saint in Pakistani Islam." PhD dissertation, University of Chicago.

Friedmann, Yohanan. *Shaykh Ahmad Sirhindi: An Outline of His Thought and a Study of His Image in the Eyes of Posterity*. Montreal: McGill-Queen's University Press, 1971.

——— *Prophecy Continuous: Aspects of Ahmadi Religious Thought and Its Medieval Background*. Berkeley: University of California Press, 1989.

——— "Ahmadiyah," in *The Oxford Encyclopedia of the Modern Islamic World*. New York: Oxford University Press, 1995.

Gilmartin, David. *Empire and Islam: Punjab and the Making of Pakistan*. Berkeley: University of California Press, 1988.

Hallaq, Wael. "Was the Gate of Ijtihad Closed?" *International Journal of Middle East Studies*, 16, 1984, pp. 3–41.

Hardy, Peter. *The Muslims of British India*. London: Cambridge University Press, 1972.

Hourani, Albert. *Arabic Thought in the Liberal Age, 1798–1939*. Cambridge: Cambridge University Press, revised edition, 1983.

Imdad Ullah Makki, Haji. *Faisla-e Haft Mas'ala*. Reprinted, with commentary by Muhammad Khalil Khan Qadri Barkati Marehrawi. Lahore: Farid Book Stall, 1406/1986.

Jones, Kenneth W. *Arya Dharm: Hindu Consciousness in 19th-Century Punjab*. Berkeley: University of California Press, 1976.

Kopf, David. *British Orientalism and the Bengal Renaissance: The Dynamics of Indian Modernization, 1773–1835*. Berkeley: University of California Press, 1969.

Lelyveld, David. *Aligarh's First Generation: Muslim Solidarity in British India*. Princeton: Princeton University Press, 1978.

Lewis, Philip. *Islamic Britain: Religion, Politics and Identity among British Muslims*. London: I.B. Tauris, 1994.

Ludden, David. *India and South Asia: A Short History*. Oxford: Oneworld, 2002.

Mahbub 'Ali Khan, Muhammad. *Buland Paya Hayat-e Hashmat 'Ali*. Kanpur: Arakin-e Bazm-e Qadiri Rizwi, 1960.

Masud, Muhammad Khalid. "Apostasy and Judicial Separation in British India," in *Islamic Legal Interpretation: Muftis and Their Fatwas*, Muhammad Khalid Masud, Brinkley Messick, and David S. Powers, eds. Cambridge: Harvard University Press, 1996.

Masud, Muhammad Khalid, Brinkley Messick, and David S. Powers, eds. *Islamic Legal Interpretation: Muftis and Their Fatwas*. Cambridge: Harvard University Press, 1996.

Metcalf, Barbara Daly. *Islamic Revival in British India: Deoband, 1860–1900*. Princeton: Princeton University Press, 1982.

——— "Two Fatwas on Hajj in British India," in *Islamic Legal Interpretation: Muftis and Their Fatwas*, Muhammad Khalid Masud, Brinkley Messick, and David S. Powers, eds. Cambridge: Harvard University Press, 1996, pp. 184–192.

Metcalf, Barbara D., and Thomas R. Metcalf. *A Concise History of India*. Cambridge: Cambridge University Press, 2002.

Metcalf, Thomas R. *Ideologies of the Raj. The New Cambridge History of*

India, vol. III.4. Cambridge: Cambridge University Press, reprint, 2001.

Mir Shahamat 'Ali, trans. "Translation of the Takwiyat-ul-Iman, Preceded by a Notice of the Author Maulavi Isma'il Hajji." *Journal of the Royal Asiatic Society*, 13 (1852), pp. 310–372.

Mushir ul-Haqq, "Unniswin Sadi ke Hindustan ki Hai'at Shar'i: Shah 'Abd ul-'Aziz ke Fatawa-e Dar al-Harb ka Ek 'Ilmi Tajzi' a." *Burhan*, 63, 4 (October 1969), pp. 221–244.

Na'imi, Ghulam Mu'in ud-Din. "Tazkira al-Ma'ruf Hayat-e Sadr al-Afazil." *Sawad-e A'zam*, vol. 2. Lahore: Na'imi Dawakhana, 1959.

Padwick, Constance E. *Muslim Devotions: A Study of Prayer-Manuals in Common Use*. Oxford: Oneworld, 1996.

Pearson, Harlan Otto. "Islamic Reform and Revival in Nineteenth Century India: The Tariqah-i Muhammadiyah." PhD dissertation, Department of History, Duke University, 1979.

Qadiri, Maulana Aulad-e Rasul. "Muhammad Miyan." *Khandan-e Barakat*. Marehra: c. 1927.

Qadiri Nuri Badayuni, Ghulam Shabbar. *Tazkira-e Nuri: Mufassal Halat o Sawanih-e Abu'l Hussain Nuri Miyan*. La'ilpur: 1968.

Qureshi, I. H. *Ulema in Politics: A Study relating to the Political Activities of the Ulema in the South Asian Subcontinent from 1556 to 1947*. Karachi: Ma'aref, 1974.

Rahman 'Ali, Maulawi. *Tazkira-e 'Ulama-e Hind*, trans. Muhammad Ayub Qadiri. Karachi: Pakistan Historical Society, no. 16, 1961.

Riza Khan, Ahmad. *Al-Dawlat al-Makkiyya bi'l Madat al-Ghaibiyya*. Karachi: Maktaba Rizwiyya, n.d.

——*Dawam al-'Aish fi'l Ummat min Quraish*. Lahore: Farid Book Stall, n.d.

——*Hada'iq-e Bakhshish*. Karachi: Medina Publishing Company, 1976.

——*Husam al-Haramain 'ala Manhar al-Kufr wa'l Main*. Lahore: Maktaba Nabawiyya, 1405/1985.

——*I'lam al-A'lam ba-an Hindustan Dar al-Islam*. Bareilly: Hasani Press, 1306/1888–9.

——*Al-Mahajjat al-Mu'tamana fi Ayat al-Mumtahana* (1339/1920). Reprinted in *Rasai'il-e Rizwiyya*, vol. 2, Lahore: Maktaba Hamidiyya, 1976.

———*Malfuzat-e A'la Hazrat*. 4 vols. Gujarat, Pakistan: Fazl-e Nur Academy, n.d.

———*Naqa al-Salafa fi Ahkam al-Bai'a wa'l Khilafa*. Sialkot, Pakistan: Maktaba Mihiriyya Rizwiyya, n.d. Originally published in 1319/1901.

———*Tadbir-e Falah wa Nijat wa Islah*. Bareilly: Hasani Press, 1331/1913.

Riza Khan, Hasnain. *Sirat-e 'Ala Hazrat*. Karachi: Maktaba Qasimiyya Barkatiyya, 1986.

Rizvi, S. A. A. *A History of Sufism in India*. Vol. 2. Delhi: Munshi Manoharlal, 1983.

Rizwi, Muhammad Hamid Siddiqi. *Takzira-e Hazrat Burhan-e Millat*. Jabalpur: Astana 'Aliyya Rizwiyya Salamiyya Burhaniyya, 1985.

Robinson, Francis. *The 'Ulama of Farangi Mahall and Islamic Culture in South Asia*. Delhi: Permanent Black, 2001.

Sanyal, Usha. "Are Wahhabis Kafirs? Ahmad Riza Khan Barelwi and His Sword of the Haramayn," in *Islamic Legal Interpretation: Muftis and Their Fatwas*, Muhammad Khalid Masud, Brinkley Messick, and David S. Powers, eds. Cambridge: Harvard University Press, 1996.

———*Devotional Islam and Politics in British India: Ahmad Riza Khan Barelwi and His Movement, 1870–1920*. Delhi: Oxford University Press, 1999.

———"Generational Changes in the Leadership of the Ahl-e Sunnat Movement in North India during the Twentieth Century." *Modern Asian Studies*, 32, 3, 1998, pp. 635–656.

Schimmel, Annemarie. *Mystical Dimensions of Islam*. Chapel Hill: University of North Carolina Press, 1975.

———*And Muhammad Is His Messenger: The Veneration of the Prophet in Islamic Piety*. Lahore: Vanguard, 1987.

Spear, Percival. *A History of India*. Vol. 2. Harmondsworth: Penguin, 1981.

Troll, Christian W. *Sayyid Ahmad Khan: A Reinterpretation of Muslim Theology*. Delhi: Vikas, 1978.

Zaman, Muhammad Qasim. *The Ulama in Contemporary Islam: Custodians of Change*. Princeton: Princeton University Press, 2002.

INDEX